The
Ultimate
PUB TRIVIA
Quiz Night
BOOK

Your life is your life,

Gotta live like it's your life

Life Is Life-Noah & The Whale

ISBN: 978-1-922409-28-7
Published by Vivid Publishing
A division of Fontaine Publishing Group
P.O. Box 948, Fremantle
Western Australia 6959
www.vividpublishing.com.au

Cataloguing-in-Publication data is available from the National Library of Australia

This book is dedicated to with much thanks and love to the people who have supported me, guided me and inspired me through my journey over the years. You know who are as I have listed you in my other books. My personal handwritten note to you is underneath.

I am indebted to them for their kind words, inspirational moments, and advice to continue when things were tough. Each one of you has made me a better person.

To the Department of Education of South Australia-whose manic obsession with meaningless and time wasting data collection, and standardised testing-especially the flawed NAPLAN and PAT tests, amongst others, destroyed my passion and love of teaching. These tests serve no educational purpose and destroy the creativity and a love of learning in students.

These clueless administrators and political hacks should listen to the words of former US President Barack Obama to understand the real meaning of what teaching and learning is all about:

"Learning is about so much more than just filling in the right bubble."

30 Things a Standardised Test Can't Measure

Resilience Passion Strength
wit Faith
Compassion
a sense of humor Intuition
Kindness self-esteem
INTELLIGENCE MOTIVATION FORTITUDE
Morals
Courage Work Ethic
empathy Determination
Personality manners
Diligence common sense
Ingenuity
Grit Character
Physical Fitness a love of learning
creativity Effort LIFE SKILLS

Introduction

Welcome to the **Ultimate Pub Trivia Quiz Night Book**. Whereas **Quiz Nights Ready to Use** and **Pub Quizzes Ready to Use** followed a similar path in the setting out of the quizzes, the **Ultimate Pub Trivia Quiz Night Book** is different in its approach.

This massive book contains **2650 NEW** trivia quiz night questions (and their answers), as well as 100 **NEW** tie breaker questions (with answers) for those really close rounds. The tie breaker questions can also be used to test people's knowledge of the really trivial in our world, or when something monumental happened.

There are **50 full quizzes** in this book, each broken down into **five rounds of 10 questions each**. This is followed by **3 bonus questions**, which are deliberately more challenging than the main quiz (unless you know the answers of course) as they can be used for bigger prizes; or if you are playing less formally, bigger bragging rights, if you get them right. As a bonus, there are also over **100 True or False** statements included for the breaks in between the rounds, or just to have fun with.

The Ultimate Pub Trivia Quiz Night Book can be used to conduct a formal quiz night, a more informal quiz session between family and friends, or just firing questions at each other. That's the beauty of this book. It has many and varied uses-you can decide how to use it. It can also be used in classrooms with older students, who should be able to answer most of the questions.

Also included are Photocopiable answer sheets for those people running a quiz night, and don't have the time to prepare one themselves. There are two versions of the answer sheets-one with a section for the bonus questions, and one without-for those choosing not to have the bonus questions as part of the quiz.

A lot of what is in this book is designed to make running a quiz night (or many quiz nights) an easy and enjoyable experience-rather than the **"Oh my God, I have to run a quiz night and I don't know where to start"** situation that many of us get caught up in. By having this book, most of the organisation has been taken care of. All the organisers have to worry about now is getting the prizes and publicity for the event.

The Ultimate Pub Trivia Quiz Night Book is designed to test people's knowledge and memory on a variety of topics. There are the obligatory easy questions which make people feel good because they can answer them quickly; the more challenging moderate questions designed for a bit more thinking, and where 'discussions' start as to who might be correct; and then some harder questions for those obscure moments in time. You'll be doing extremely well if you score full marks in the quizzes, plus the Bonus Round questions, and even the tie-breaker questions. In that case, you are well qualified to write your own quiz book.

The Ultimate Pub Trivia Quiz Night Book continues the passion for quizzes and is designed in an easy to read format, and just as importantly, finding the answers quickly. Answers to both rounds, and the Bonus Questions are at the end of each quiz; not all tucked in at the end of the book where finding answers can become an unnecessary time-wasting chore. All the tie breaker questions are at the end of the book with the answers next to the question in bold letters; again, designed for a quick reference.

I hope you enjoy the challenge, fun, frustration and even team spirit of **The Ultimate Pub Trivia Quiz Night Book.**

May all your answers be correct!!

Tom Trifonoff

Quiz 1

Round 1

1. How many stories did each of the World Trade Towers have?
2. In what year was Barack Obama born?
3. Who did Ted Turner, the media tycoon, marry in 1991?
4. By what name was Helen Porter Mitchell better known?
5. The doomed ship Titanic had two sister ships. What were their names?
6. Still in use today, which country's flag is the oldest in the world?
7. Which country contains the largest number of active volcanoes?
8. What is the collective term for a group of racehorses?
9. What is the capital of North Korea?
10. What name was given to the Chinese peasant uprising of 1900?

Round 2

1. Which series of horror films take place in the fictional town of Springwood, Ohio?
2. Who sang the first line of the USA for Africa's 'We Are the World'?
3. How many world title fights did Mohammed Ali contest under the name of Cassius Clay?
4. In `The Lone Ranger` what was Tonto's horse called?
5. Who had a hit single with `Werewolves of London`?
6. Who painted 'The Umbrellas'?
7. How many men have walked on the moon?
8. Which famous actor had a small role in 'Robin Hood: Prince of Thieves' and donated his fee for the film to charity?
9. In which year did Disney Land first open in California? 1955, 1960 or 1965?
10. How many rounds are there in an amateur boxing match?

Round 3

1. How many paintings did Vincent Van Gogh sell during his life?
2. How many Oscar nominations did Titanic receive?
3. In 1967, who appeared on the first cover of Rolling Stone magazine?
4. On which planet in the Solar System does it constantly rain acid?
5. The first ever Commonwealth games were held in which country?
6. What was Bill Clinton's original surname? Bunton, Blunt or Blythe?
7. Which of the following English King`s never married? William II, Edward II or George II?
8. In 'The Simpsons', what is the name of Ned Flanders wife?
9. Easter Island is a dependency of which country?
10. The film 'Chariots of Fire' is based around the Olympics of what year?

Round 4

1. Which European country began the tradition of exchanging gifts at Christmas time?
2. In what year did Marilyn Monroe die?
3. Who was the second President of the USA?
4. What is the singular of the word 'graffiti'?
5. Who is the only TV cartoon dog to have an Antarctic island named after him?
6. Who was the first English monarch to be addressed as 'Your Majesty'?
7. In what year did the Beatles officially split up?
8. What is a female donkey called?
9. What does 5 on the Beaufort Scale represent? A fresh breeze, a light breeze or a near gale?
10. Which of the following Mr. Men are red in colour? Mr Nonsense, Mr Greedy or Mr Bump?

Round 5

1. In which European country was tennis player Monica Seles born?
2. In 1985, what was Robert Ballard famous for discovering?
3. Diamond is the birthstone for which month?
4. What is the ruling planet of the astrological sign Sagittarius?
5. In which country did the card game baccarat originate?
6. From 1976, how many successive Wimbledon titles did Bjorn Borg win?
7. Which famous actor anonymously entered a look-alike contest for himself in Monaco, and came third?
8. In `Finding Nemo` what is the name of Nemo's dad who is looking for him?
9. Which of the following elements has the highest atomic number? Lead, Xenon or Zirconium?
10. How many days is the average gestation period of a rabbit? 30, 50 or 70?

Quiz One-Bonus Round Questions
1. What year was the first motor race held that was classed as Formula 1?
2. According to the BBC how many rooms are there in Buckingham Palace?
3. Who created Wikipedia on the World Wide Web?

Answers Quiz One

Round 1

1. 110
2. 1961
3. Jane Fonda
4. Dame Nellie Melba
5. Britannic and Olympic
6. Denmark`s
7. Indonesia
8. A string of racehorses
9. Pyongyang
10. Boxer Rebellion

Round 2

1. Nightmare on Elm Street
2. Lionel Ritchie
3. One
4. Scout
5. Warren Zevon
6. Renoir
7. 12
8. Sean Connery
9. 1955
10. 3

Round 3

1. 1
2. 14
3. John Lennon
4. Venus
5. Canada
6. Blythe
7. William II
8. Maude
9. Chile
10. 1924

Round 4

1. Italy
2. 1962
3. John Adams
4. Graffito
5. Huckleberry Hound
6. Henry VIII
7. 1970
8. A jenny
9. Fresh breeze
10. Mr Greedy

Round 5

1. Yugoslavia
2. The Titanic
3. April
4. Jupiter
5. France
6. Five
7. Charlie Chaplin
8. Marlin
9. Lead
10. 30

Quiz One-Bonus Round Answers

1. 1950
2. 775
3. Jimmy Wales

Quiz 2

Round 1

1. A tangelo is a cross between a tangerine and which other fruit?
2. What is the more common name for tauromancy?
3. In the Roman Catholic Church what is the title given to a person who is appointed to oppose a candidate's claim for canonisation?
4. What was the first product advertised on Britain's Channel 5?
5. Which book of the Bible chronicles the birth of Moses?
6. When Brazil won the World Cup in 1994, which sports star did they dedicate their victory to?
7. In the human body, where is the canthus?
8. How many states of the US begin with the letter M?
9. Who established the Sundance Film Festival?
10. Which pop star was stabbed in the eye with a compass when he was a London schoolboy?

Round 2

1. Peter II was the last king of which European country?
2. What is the only English anagram of the word alarming?
3. What is the edible nickname of the US state of Idaho?
4. Who played the character Ted Bullpitt in the TV series 'Kingswood Country'?
5. What kind of projectile was depicted on the Sydney Olympic torches?
6. Which US basketball team are known as the Trailblazers?
7. What are there 33 of in the human body?
8. In which city is the world's largest palace?
9. Which Australian city stands at the head of Port Phillip Bay?
10. Which actor was born Ramon Estevez in 1940?

Round 3

1. Which American football team is known as the Colts?
2. On what date was Donald Trump inaugurated as US President?
3. Who was born on Daisy Hill Puppy Farm?
4. What is latitude 66 degrees north more commonly known as?
5. What is traditionally given on a 13th wedding anniversary?
6. What is the first name of Granny in 'The Beverly Hillbillies'?
7. In the 'Jungle Book', what type of creature is Mang?
8. In which city is the WACA cricket stadium?
9. Which novel is narrated by Nick Carraway?
10. Kookaburras belong to which bird family?

Round 4

1. What is the fastest growing member of the grass family?
2. What is celebrated on the third Sunday of June in the USA?
3. Which king was responsible for the Massacre of the Innocents?
4. Which pop star was named Man of the Year in 1985?
5. In which city was the peace treaty signed that marked the end of the Vietnam War?
6. By what name is the rock guitarist Dave Evans better known?
7. In what decade did Constantinople change its name to Istanbul?
8. In which month does United Nations Day fall?
9. Who first played the Australian soap character Scott Robinson?
10. In which city was Robinson Crusoe born?

Round 5

1. Which song opens with the line, 'Picture yourself on a boat on a river'?
2. Which South American capital city is also a variety of bean?
3. Which bone in the human body is named after the Italian word for flute?
4. What does a graphologist study?
5. In which desert does the city of Las Vegas lie?
6. What is the world's highest island?
7. Which co-producer of the film 'Chariots of Fire' died in a car crash in 1997?
8. Which pop group named themselves after a sports centre in Swindon, England?
9. In 1989, which country changed its name to Myanmar?
10. 10 Mathew Street is the address of which famous musical location?

Quiz Two-Bonus Round Questions

1. What is the deepest lake in the world?
2. How many Popes have been assassinated?
3. Who played Friar Tuck in the film 'Robin and Marian'?

Answers Quiz Two

Round 1

1. Grapefruit
2. Bull fighting
3. Devils' Advocate
4. Chanel No. 5
5. Exodus
6. Ayrton Senna
7. Corner of the eye
8. 8
9. Robert Redford
10. David Bowie

Round 2

1. Yugoslavia
2. Marginal
3. The potato state
4. Ross Higgins
5. Boomerang
6. Portland
7. Vertebrae
8. Beijing
9. Melbourne
10. Martin Sheen

Round 3

1. Indianapolis
2. January 20th 2017
3. Snoopy
4. Arctic Circle
5. Lace
6. Daisy
7. A bat
8. Perth
9. The Great Gatsby
10. Kingfisher

Round 4

1. Bamboo
2. Father's Day
3. King Herod
4. Bob Geldof
5. Paris
6. The Edge
7. 1930s
8. October
9. Jason Donovan
10. York

Round 5

1. Lucy in the sky with Diamonds
2. Lima
3. Tibia
4. Handwriting
5. Mojave Desert
6. New Guinea
7. Dodi Al Fayed
8. Oasis
9. Burma
10. Cavern Club

Quiz Two-Bonus Round Answers

1. Lake Baikal
2. 26
3. Ronnie Barker

Quiz 3

Round 1

1. Which US state is named on the label of a Jack Daniels bottle?
2. What type of animal was inside Sputnik 2 when launched into orbit in 1957?
3. What type of creature is a dugite?
4. Who painted The Water Lily Pool?
5. Who wrote the book Catch-22?
6. Kodiak Island is in which US state?
7. What is the name of Moe's pet cat in the cartoon show The Simpsons?
8. What drink is named from old German meaning swallow?
9. What is the largest planet in the Solar System?
10. By what name do we now know the islands previously called the Danish West Indies?

Round 2

1. In years, what is the length of term for a French President?
2. Who did Novak Djokovic defeat in the Australian Open final of 2008 to win his first major Grand Slam tennis title?
3. In which North American city do the "Pirates" play baseball and the "Penguins", ice hockey?
4. Who provided the voice of Jessica Rabbit in the movie "Who Framed Roger Rabbit"?
5. In which country would you find "Alexander the Great Airport"?
6. What is the name of the Griffin family's talking dog in the TV series "Family Guy"?
7. Who is the only player to have won all four tennis grand prix men's singles in one season twice?
8. Who was the last of the Tudor monarchs to rule England?
9. In which US State did the first detonation of a nuclear device take place in July 1945?
10. Which was the first city in the Southern Hemisphere to host the Summer Olympic Games?

Round 3

1. Which West Indian batsman became in 2012 the first player to hit a six off the first ball of a test match?
2. What is the capital of Bosnia-Herzegovina?
3. Which best-selling rock band's name originated from the change given at a Starbucks coffee Shop?
4. Extending from the lumbar and sacral plexuses in the back to the thighs, which is the longest nerve in the human body?

5. Which instrument was played by American jazz musician Gene Krupa?
6. Which country is home to the chicken restaurant chain, Nando's?
7. In which US city is the baseball stadium Fenway Park located?
8. Which fictional continent is the main setting for TV's "Game of Thrones"?
9. What name is given to the Sunday prior to Easter Sunday?
10. Who provided the voice of the title character in the 2009 animation "Fantastic Mr Fox"?

Round 4

1. Which fictional character was known as "The Demon Barber of Fleet Street"?
2. What organisation was founded by George Williams in London on June 6th 1844?
3. How many hearts does an octopus have?
4. Of which country is Cape Farewell the southernmost point?
5. In which German city would you find the headquarters of the BMW car company?
6. Which stringed instrument is played with a metallic pick called a Mizraab?
7. Which modern day country was once known as Upper Peru?
8. Which vitamin is also known as Riboflavin?
9. How many strings are there on a standard Mandolin?
10. Who is the only US President who is depicted on Mount Rushmore but does not feature on a banknote?

Round 5

1. What illness is caused by the Epstein-Barr virus?
2. What metal is obtained from the ore Bauxite?
3. In computing for what does the acronym JPEG stand?
4. What is pop superstar Rihanna's real surname?
5. What is the capital of Queensland?
6. Which synthetic fibre used in tyres and body armour was developed by Stephanie Kwolek in 1965?
7. Formed during the Irish War of Independence, by what nickname are the Royal Irish Constabulary Reserve Force better known as?
8. Which band had hit albums in the 1980s entitled "Back in Black" and "Blow Up Your Video"?
9. Which book of the Bible tells the story of Samson and Delilah?
10. The name of which disease is derived from the Medieval Italian for "Bad Air"?

Quiz Three-Bonus Round Questions

1. In which year was the website google.com first registered?
2. On which fictional island is the BBC series "Death in Paradise" set?
3. Which everyday object was invented by Walter Hunt in 1849?

Answers Quiz Three

Round 1

1. Tennessee
2. Dog
3. Snake
4. Claude Monet
5. Joseph Heller
6. Alaska
7. Mr Snookums
8. Schnapps
9. Jupiter
10. The Virgin Islands

Round 2

1. Five years
2. Jo-Wilfred Tsonga
3. Pittsburgh
4. Kathleen Turner
5. North Macedonia
6. Brian
7. Rod Laver (1962, 1969)
8. Queen Elizabeth I
9. New Mexico
10. Melbourne Australia

Round 3

1. Chris Gayle
2. Sarajevo
3. Nickleback
4. The sciatic nerve
5. Drums
6. South Africa
7. Boston
8. Westeros
9. Palm Sunday
10. George Clooney

Round 4

1. Sweeney Todd
2. YMCA
3. Three
4. Greenland
5. Munich
6. Sitar
7. Bolivia
8. Vitamin B2
9. Eight (Four pairs)
10. Theodore Roosevelt

Round 5

1. Glandular Fever
2. Aluminium
3. Joint Photographic Experts Group
4. Fenty
5. Brisbane
6. Kevlar
7. Black & Tans
8. AC/DC
9. Judges
10. Malaria

Quiz Three-Bonus Round Answers

1. (September 15th) 1997
2. Saint-Marie
3. Safety Pin

Quiz 4

Round 1

1. How many moons does the planet Mercury have?
2. For which baseball team did both Joe DiMaggio and Babe Ruth play?
3. Who was the Roman God of the Sea?
4. On which Caribbean island did Calypso music originate?
5. Used generally in the cooking of lamb, which herb is thought to be the herb of remembrance?
6. What is the term used to describe a dry champagne?
7. In which city was Archduke Franz Ferdinand assassinated?
8. What breed of dog is Scooby Doo?
9. The characters Mrs White and Colonel Mustard appear in the standard version of which board game?
10. How many atoms of oxygen are contained in a water molecule?

Round 2

1. What is the name of the bear in Kipling's "The Jungle Book"?
2. Who wrote the book "How the Grinch Stole Christmas"?
3. Sergei Bubka was an Olympic champion in which sport?
4. What are the horizontal rows of the Periodic Table called?
5. Which famous golfer was instrumental in starting the US Masters and helped to design the course?
6. In which city were the war trials held after the Second World War?
7. What sport features in the 1992 film "A League of Their Own"?
8. Who created the character of Peter Pan?
9. Which former pop star was elected mayor of Palm Springs in April 1988?
10. What are the halls decked with in the well-known Christmas carol?

Round 3

1. Which word goes before vest, beans and quartet?
2. Which planet is the furthest away from the Sun?
3. Which two metals combine to form brass?
4. What size paper is half an A4 sheet?
5. Which salad was named after a New York hotel?
6. In degrees what do the angles in a triangle add up to?
7. Which US playwright wrote both "Death of a Salesman" and "The Crucible"?
8. Which wrestler starred in the 1996 film "Santa with Muscles"?
9. What is the young of a penguin called?
10. In which year did Adolf Hitler become the German Fuhrer?

Round 4

1. Which car manufacturer makes the Lexus line of cars?
2. What relation was King George II to King George III?
3. Which 1965 Bob Dylan song was listed at Number 1 of "The Greatest Songs of all Time" by Rolling Stone magazine?
4. Who wrote the book entitled "A Brief History of Time"?
5. What was the name of the car driven by Luke and Bo Duke in TV's "The Dukes of Hazard"?
6. Which country has won the most Olympic medals since 1896?
7. From whose garden did Peter Rabbit steal vegetables against the strict instruction from his mother?
8. Who discovered Calisto & Ganymede, two of Jupiter's moons?
9. Which European country has the largest number of volcanos?
10. What is someone who shoes horses called?

Round 5

1. In music, what do the letters ARIA stand for?
2. Who was the director of the Lord of the Rings trilogy?
3. Who played Neo in The Matrix?
4. Name the actress whose career began at the age of 3, and who went on to star in films such as Contact, Maverick and The Silence of the Lambs?
5. Which sport does Constantino Rocca play?
6. Which chess piece can only move diagonally?
7. How many valves does a trumpet have?
8. Who was the Australian Prime Minister in 1995?
9. In publishing, what does POD mean?
10. What flavour is Cointreau?

Quiz Four-Bonus Round Questions

1. In what year did the music show 'Countdown' begin in Australia?
2. How many mystery novels did Agatha Christie write?
3. Who is the only footballer to have played for Liverpool, Everton, Manchester City and Manchester United?

Answers Quiz Four

Round 1

1. None
2. New York Yankees
3. Neptune
4. Trinidad
5. Rosemary
6. Brut
7. Sarajevo
8. Great Dane
9. Cluedo
10. One

Round 2

1. Baloo
2. Dr Seuss
3. Pole vault
4. Periods
5. Bobby Jones
6. Nuremburg
7. (Women's) baseball
8. J M Barrie
9. Sonny Bono
10. Boughs of holly

Round 3

1. String
2. Neptune
3. Copper and zinc
4. A5
5. Waldorf salad
6. 180
7. Arthur Miller
8. Hulk Hogan
9. A chick
10. 1934

Round 4

1. Toyota
2. Grandfather
3. Like a Rolling Stone
4. Stephen Hawking
5. General Lee
6. USA
7. Mr McGregor
8. Galileo
9. Iceland
10. A farmer

Round 5

1. Australian Recording Industry Association
2. Peter Jackson
3. Keanu Reeves
4. Jodie Foster
5. Golf
6. A bishop
7. Three
8. Paul Keating
9. Print on Demand
10. Orange

Quiz Four-Bonus Round Answers

1. 1974
2. 78
3. Peter Beardsley

Quiz 5

Round 1

1. How many colours are there in a rainbow?
2. What is a large marquee called when used to house a circus?
3. What do you call a time span of one thousand years?
4. How many degrees are found in a circle?
5. The Dewey Decimal system is used to categorise what?
6. How many squares are there on a chess board?
7. Who is Norma Jean Baker more famously known as?
8. What is the Scottish drink made from whisky and heather honey called?
9. What life-saving device did Sir Humphrey Davy invent?
10. Who was the legendary king who was killed at the Battle of Camelford?

Round 2

1. How many points does a compass have in total?
2. Who composed the music for the ballets Sleeping Beauty and Swan Lake?
3. Who was known as The Tramp or The King of Comedy?
4. In Japanese, what is the word for goodbye?
5. How many American cents make up a dime?
6. What is the Chinese game played with small tiles called?
7. What do you call the smell which wine gives off?
8. Whose statue in Red Square was pulled down in 1991?
9. How many strings does a cello have?
10. In which year did Australia start using the decimal currency?

Round 3

1. Which former American President had a popular children's toy named after him?
2. What is rum distilled from?
3. What nationality of soldiers wears a white kilt?
4. Which fictional character was also known as Lord Greystoke?
5. Who wrote The Grapes of Wrath?
6. How many sides does a dodecagon have?
7. How many symphonies did Beethoven compose?
8. Who was the Spartan king who married Helen of Troy?
9. What are tarot cards usually used for?
10. What sort of animals feature in the children's book, Watership Down?

Round 4

1. Which branch of mathematics deals with the sides and angles of triangles, and their relationship to each other?
2. What collective noun is given to the first 10 amendments of the US Constitution?
3. In the Marvel comics, Dr Don Blake is the secret identity of which superhero?
4. Which movie studio released The Jazz Singer, the first talking film?
5. Who was Prime Minister of Australia when colour TV commenced?
6. The line, 'All the world's a stage' appears in which Shakespeare play?
7. The term 'highly strung' originated in which sport?
8. Which planet was discovered in in 1846?
9. Galapago is the Spanish name for which animal?
10. Which country won four boxing gold medals at the 1996 Olympic Games?

Round 5

1. In 'The Lord of the Rings', who is the maker of the ring?
2. The US Medal of Honour depicts which goddess?
3. Which country was divided by the 38th Parallel in 1945?
4. Which actor narrated the TV series 'Walking with Dinosaurs?
5. In which country did the 'Punch and Judy' shows originate?
6. Who was the last Australian Prime Minister before Tony Abbott?
7. Who was the first duo inducted into the Rock and Roll Hall of Fame?
8. What was the first organisation to win the Nobel Peace Prize twice?
9. What is the largest brass instrument?
10. Which was the first team to win back-to back VFL/AFL Premierships?

Quiz Five-Bonus Round Questions

1. In which year did Queen Victoria celebrate her Diamond Jubilee?
2. What was the last major battle of WW2?
3. How many AFL/VFL Premierships did the now defunct team Fitzroy win?

Answers Quiz Five

Round 1

1. 7
2. Big Top
3. Millennium
4. 360
5. Books
6. 64
7. Marilyn Monroe
8. Drambuie
9. Miner's safety lamp
10. Arthur

Round 2

1. 32
2. Tchaikovsky
3. Charlie Chaplin
4. Sayonara
5. 10
6. Mah-Jong
7. Bouquet
8. Lenin's
9. 4
10. 1966

Round 3

1. Theodore Roosevelt
2. Sugar cane
3. Greek
4. Tarzan
5. John Steinbeck
6. 12
7. 9
8. Menelaus
9. Fortune telling
10. Rabbits

Round 4

1. Trigonometry
2. The Bill of Rights
3. Mighty Thor
4. Warner Brothers
5. Gough Whitlam
6. As You Like It
7. Archery
8. Neptune
9. Tortoise
10. Cuba

Round 5

1. Sauron the Great
2. Minerva
3. Korea
4. Kenneth Branagh
5. Italy
6. Kevin Rudd
7. The Everly Brothers
8. The International Red Cross
9. Tuba
10. Collingwood

Quiz Five-Bonus Round Answers

1. 1897
2. The Battle of Okinawa
3. 8

Quiz 6

Round 1

1. Who was the eldest of the Marx Brothers?
2. In the human body what is the hallux?
3. Port Said is in which North African country?
4. Which country is known as the Pearl of Africa?
5. Playing music/video online in 'real time' without downloading is called?
6. In which year of the 20th century did the United Kingdom have three Kings?
7. Which piece of gardening equipment was invented by James Ransome in 1902?
8. In which city was the term Ghetto originally used?
9. Known as "The King of Swing", what instrument was played by band leader Benny Goodman?
10. Who in 1949 became the first Prime Minister of Israel?

Round 2

1. What is the capital of Bosnia-Herzegovina?
2. What is the capital of the Northern Territory?
3. Who became President of the European Commission in November 2019?
4. In which town did Superman grow up in before moving to Metropolis?
5. In Greek mythology who killed Achilles?
6. Who were the 2015 winners of baseball's World Series?
7. What was the occupation of Cliff Clavin in the TV sit-com "Cheers"?
8. How many days after Easter Sunday does Pentecost fall?
9. From which country did Madagascar gain independence in 1960?
10. Which fruit is used to make the Eastern European spirit Slivovitz?

Round 3

1. In the TV series "The Man from UNCLE" who was the boss of Napoleon Solo and Ilya Kuryakin?
2. Of which Australian state was Joan Kirner a Premier?
3. With a gestation period of 640 days which mammal has the longest pregnancy?
4. Whose first 'secret diary' was written when he was 13 and three-quarters?
5. Which 60s performer was known as "The Godfather of Soul"?
6. In which English city did Roger Bannister break the "Four Minute Mile" in 1954?
7. In which Australian state are the Mt Lofty Ranges?
8. What was the last musical to be written by Rodgers and Hammerstein?
9. Which was the third country to have a man in space?
10. Who was Fred Astaire's female co-star in the 1948 movie "Easter Parade"?

Round 4

1. What does the word "SAHARA" mean in Arabic?
2. Who was the arch-enemy of Sherlock Holmes?
3. How often do teams compete for golf's The Ryder Cup?
4. In which Australian state is the town of Meekatharra?
5. What colour is the five-pointed star on the Morocco flag?
6. What six letter word is the name given to the frozen treeless plains of the Arctic Circle?
7. What colour are emu's eggs?
8. In which city is Kingsford Smith International Airport?
9. In 1993, Kim Campbell became the first female Prime Minister of which country?
10. What four words first appeared on US coins in 1864 and were adapted into a motto 82 years later?

Round 5

1. What is phasmophobia the fear of?
2. What sauce usually covers the dish Eggs Benedict?
3. The film 'The Miracle Worker' chronicled the life story of which lady?
4. By what other name is the creature the Goanna known by?
5. What piece of sporting equipment has a maximum width of 10.8 cm?
6. From which country did pheasants originate?
7. Varig was the national airline of which South American country?
8. Which Nazi was nicknamed the Angel of Death?
9. Which was the first cartoon group to have a No. 1 hit?
10. Who was Premier of New South Wales when the Sydney Harbour Bridge was opened?

Quiz Six-Bonus Round Questions

1. In which year did Damon Hill win the Formula One World Championship?
2. Where did the Great Fire of London end?
3. How many bouts did boxer Mohammed Ali win in his professional career prior to his first defeat in 1971?

Answers Quiz Six

Round 1

1. Chico
2. Big toe
3. Egypt
4. Uganda
5. Streaming
6. 1936
7. Lawn Mower
8. Venice
9. Clarinet
10. David Ben-Gurion

Round 2

1. Sarajevo
2. Darwin
3. Ursula von der Leyen
4. Smallville
5. Paris
6. Kansas City Royals
7. Postman
8. 50
9. France
10. Plums

Round 3

1. Mr Waverly
2. Victoria
3. African elephant
4. Adrian Mole
5. James Brown
6. Oxford
7. South Australia
8. The Sound of Music
9. Czechoslovakia
10. Judy Garland

Round 4

1. Desert
2. Professor Moriarty
3. Every two years
4. Western Australia
5. Green
6. Tundra
7. Green
8. Sydney
9. Canada
10. In God we Trust

Round 5

1. Ghosts
2. Hollandaise
3. Helen Keller
4. Monitor
5. Cricket bat
6. China
7. Brazil
8. Josef Mengele
9. The Archies
10. Jack Lang

Quiz Six-Bonus Round Answers

1. 1996
2. Pie Corner
3. 31

Quiz 7

Round 1

1. Which character does Morgan Freeman play in Bruce Almighty?
2. What letter is located between letters X and V on a standard keyboard?
3. How many megabytes are there in 1 gigabyte?
4. As of 2019, which swimmer had won the most Olympic medals?
5. Who is lead singer of the Foo Fighters?
6. What is the tallest breed of dog in the world?
7. Who is the author of The Hunger Games trilogy?
8. Which actor starred in: What Lies Beneath, Six Days and Seven Nights and Air Force One?
9. What does the Olympic motto 'Citius, Altius, Fortius' mean?
10. With reference to mobile phone networks, what does 3G stand for?

Round 2

1. If you were born on the 29th October, which star sign would you belong to?
2. Which tree produces conkers?
3. The crosses of St George, St Patrick, and St Andrew make up which flag?
4. In the 2009 film 'The Hangover' which Las Vegas hotel did the bachelor party stay at?
5. What is the highest number visible on a dart board?
6. Which breed of dog is believed to be the fastest?
7. Who was the author of Peter Rabbit?
8. Who had a 1980s hit with the song entitled '99 Red Balloons'?
9. How many ribs are in a human body?
10. Which continents form the New World?

Round 3

1. In Roald Dahl's famous book, what do the letters BFG stand for?
2. If 'on the rocks' is stated on a drinks menu, what is meant by this?
3. What is the longest river in England that runs through England only?
4. In the film E.T. who played the role of Elliott's little sister Gertie?
5. Which well-known brand uses the motto 'Just Do It'?
6. Who had a 1960 hit with the song 'Save the Last Dance for Me'?
7. Which country is known as the Land of White Elephant?
8. What is the name of the very small Japanese tree that is grown in a pot?
9. What is the name of the longest snake in the world?
10. Which famous musical featured the song 'You've Got to Pick a Pocket or Two'?

Round 4

1. On a roulette wheel, what colour is zero?
2. What does DVD stand for?
3. Which brothers flew the first powered aircraft?
4. During which year did the Lockerbie disaster occur?
5. What is the smallest ocean in the world?
6. Who had a 1990's hit with the song 'Bump N' Grind'?
7. Who was the Premier of South Australia after Don Dunstan in 1979?
8. Which tennis player won two women's Grand Slam Tournaments in one year five different times?
9. Which planet is closest to the sun?
10. Which colour eyes do more humans have?

Round 5

1. Which two parts of the body continue to grow for your entire life?
2. How many millimetres are there in 3.75 meters?
3. According to the song, what did Molly Malone sell on the streets of Dublin?
4. What was the Luftwaffe?
5. What measurement is abbreviated to tsp?
6. Who wrote the novel entitled 'Les Miserables'?
7. What type of food is a yam?
8. How many points is the green ball worth in snooker?
9. Which breed of dog played Lassie in the famous movie?
10. What colour is the tongue of a giraffe?

Quiz Seven-Bonus Round Questions

1. Outside which New York building was John Lennon killed?
2. In which year did England and Wales become united with Scotland?
3. How many episodes were there of the soap opera Number 96?

Answers Quiz Seven

Round 1

1. God
2. Letter C
3. 1000
4. Michael Phelps
5. Dave Grohl
6. The Great Dane
7. Suzanne Collins
8. Harrison Ford
9. Faster, Higher, Stronger
10. 3rd generation

Round 2

1. Scorpio
2. Chestnut tree
3. The Union Jack
4. Caesar's Palace
5. Twenty
6. The greyhound
7. Beatrix Potter
8. Nena
9. Twenty four
10. North America and South America

Round 3

1. Big Friendly Giant
2. Served with ice
3. The Thames
4. Drew Barrymore
5. Nike
6. The Drifters
7. Thailand
8. Bonsai Tree
9. Python
10. Oliver!

Round 4

1. Green
2. Digital Versatile Disc
3. Wright Brothers
4. 1988
5. The Arctic
6. R Kelly
7. Des Corcoran
8. Chris Evert-Lloyd
9. Mercury
10. Brown

Round 5

1. The nose and ears
2. 3750mm
3. Cockles and mussels
4. The German Air Force
5. Teaspoon
6. Victor Hugo
7. Sweet potato
8. Three
9. Collie
10. Blue

Quiz Seven-Bonus Round Answers

1. Dakota
2. 1707
3. 1218

Quiz 8

Round 1

1. How many moons has the planet Neptune got?
2. What is the minimum amount of games required to play to win a set in tennis?
3. What is the capital of Jordan?
4. Which song did Bruce Springsteen win an Oscar for?
5. What is the only muscle in the body that is attached at one end?
6. Which dinosaur ate plants and had spiky plates along its back?
7. In which city was Anne Frank's hiding place?
8. What sort of shop did the Great fire of London break out in 1666?
9. How many sides does a heptagon have?
10. What is the most popular sport throughout the world?

Round 2

1. What is the largest type of deer?
2. How many years is a term of presidency at the White House?
3. Complete the saying "Honesty is.....
4. What unit of measurement is used to identify the height of a horse?
5. Eagles, Kestrels and Buzzards are all types of what species?
6. How many red and white stripes are there on the flag of the United States of America?
7. Lacharophobia is a fear of what food?
8. Which female American singer shaved her head in 2007?
9. What type of animal is Skippy?
10. What year did the Titanic sink after hitting an iceberg?

Round 3

1. How many pounds (lbs.) are there in 1 stone?
2. What is the capital of Finland?
3. Which author wrote the Chronicles of Narnia?
4. What type of angle has less than 90 degrees?
5. In which UK city was the 1997 movie The Full Monty set?
6. Besides fingers and toes, what other human body part has unique prints?
7. Which robot was CP30's partner in Star Wars?
8. Who was known as the Crocodile Hunter from Australia?
9. Peter Andre used to be married to which famous model?
10. Which Christmas poem includes the lyrics 'not a creature was stirring'?

Round 4

1. Which country presented the Statue of Liberty to America as a gift?
2. What has the chemical symbol H20?
3. In what year did World War Two end?
4. What word can refer to a country, a type of meat or three consecutive strikes in bowling?
5. Which two people were told never to leave the Garden of Eden?
6. Including the white ball, how many colour varieties are used in a game of snooker?
7. Which body part can be placed before the following words: drum, ache, ring?
8. Which animal comes first in the English dictionary?
9. Which continent has no active volcanoes?
10. What is a group of ravens otherwise known as?

Round 5

1. By what name is an orca more commonly known?
2. British stamps are different to any other stamps in the world as they are the only ones to not bear what?
3. Which soft drink did John Pemberton invent?
4. What year did the American Civil War start?
5. Which American state ends with three vowels?
6. How many Bond themes did Shirley Bassey sing?
7. How many days are there in a leap year?
8. Which is the only body organ able to regenerate itself?
9. Tin Lizzie is a nickname for which automobile?
10. What are the three primary colours?

Quiz Eight-Bonus Round Questions

1. In what year did Madonna release her song 'Like a Virgin'?
2. What famous girl group was originally known as 'The Primettes'?
3. Which disease did Christiaan Eijkman discover the cause of in 1897?

Answers Quiz Eight

Round 1

1. 14
2. Six
3. Amman
4. Streets of Philadelphia
5. The tongue
6. Stegosaurus
7. Amsterdam
8. A baker's shop
9. Seven
10. Football (soccer)

Round 2

1. The moose
2. Four
3. The best policy
4. Hands
5. Birds
6. 13 stripes
7. Vegetables
8. Britney Spears
9. Kangaroo
10. 1912

Round 3

1. 14
2. Helsinki
3. C S Lewis
4. Acute
5. Sheffield
6. The tongue
7. R2D2
8. Steve Irwin
9. Katie Price
10. The Night Before Christmas

Round 4

1. France
2. Water
3. 1945
4. Turkey
5. Adam & Eve
6. Eight
7. Ear
8. Aardvark
9. Australia
10. Unkindness

Round 5

1. Killer whale
2. The name of the country
3. Coca Cola
4. 1861
5. Hawaii
6. Three
7. 366
8. Liver
9. Model T Ford
10. Red, yellow, blue

Quiz Eight-Bonus Round Answers

1. 1984
2. The Supremes
3. Beriberi

Quiz 9

Round 1

1. Who is the author of 'Lady Chatterley's Lover'?
2. What is a balalaika?
3. Who released an album called 'E=MC²'?
4. Which James Bond movie is an anagram of 'cosyspout'?
5. What 'M' is the name given to a conductor of classical music?
6. Besides Ohio, which other US states begins with the letter "O"?
7. What are twisters and cyclones also known as?
8. Many tourists travel to which country to climb Mount Kilimanjaro?
9. Which leisure activity is associated with 10 pins and strikes?
10. What are the first names of ice skaters Torvil and Dean?

Round 2

1. What is the primary religion in Thailand?
2. What is the opening line to the 2014 song 'Happy' by Pharrell Williams?
3. Complete the saying 'A picture is worth...'?
4. Dos is Spanish for which number?
5. How many days are there between Halloween and Christmas (excluding the days on which they fall)?
6. What is the last letter of the Greek alphabet?
7. How many hours are equal to 600 minutes?
8. Which continent does Cyprus belong to?
9. What V makes up the spinal column?
10. A mule is the offspring of which two animals?

Round 3

1. What is the meaning of the Latin phrase 'bona fide'?
2. Which word can be placed before the following words to create well known phrases: man, bag, and box?
3. The Romans regarded Jupiter, the king of gods, as the equivalent of which Greek god?
4. What do the fifty stars on the US flag represent:
5. What is the square root of 100?
6. Which brand of chocolate claims to 'melt in your mouth, not in your hand'?
7. Which two oceans are connected by the Panama Canal via the Caribbean Sea?
8. Which avenue is the Empire State Building located on?
9. Sally Ride was the first American woman to do what?
10. Which vitamin can humans obtain from sunlight?

Round 4

1. The tense relationship that occurred between the three main powers (United States, Soviet Union, United Kingdom) following World War II was known as what war?
2. What famous prison is located on an island in San Francisco Bay?
3. How many incisor teeth are there in a full set of adult teeth?
4. What letter is located between the letters A and D on a standard keyboard?
5. What is a supernova?
6. What is the biggest country by area in North America?
7. What name is given to hot fluid below the Earth's crust from which lava is formed?
8. What was the name of the space mission that landed the first humans on the moon?
9. Which major river flows through London?
10. What was the first Pirates of the Caribbean movie called?

Round 5

1. What is the main language spoken in New Zealand?
2. Which school did Harry Potter attend?
3. How many strings are there on a banjo?
4. How many daughters does Barack Obama have?
5. Cantaloupe is a well-known variety of what?
6. Which planet is closest to the Earth?
7. Which era occurred first, the Stone Age or the Bronze Age?
8. True or false: The temperature on the moon is roughly the same all day?
9. What is the centre point (neutral) of the PH scale?
10. What is represented by the seven spikes on the Statue of Liberty's crown?

Quiz Nine-Bonus Round Questions

1. What did Robert G. Heft design as part of a school project in 1958?
2. How many American flags remain standing on the moon?
3. What is the main commercial airport serving the Las Vegas Valley?

Answers Quiz Nine

Round 1

1. D.H. Lawrence
2. A stringed musical instrument
3. Mariah Carey
4. Octopussy
5. Maestro
6. Oklahoma
7. Tornadoes
8. Tanzania
9. Ten pin bowling
10. Jayne Torvil and Christopher Dean

Round 2

1. Buddhism
2. It might seem crazy what I'm about to say
3. A thousand words
4. Number two
5. Fifty four days
6. Omega
7. Ten hours
8. Europe
9. Vertebrae
10. (Male) donkey and (female) horse

Round 3

1. In good faith
2. Post
3. Zeus
4. The states
5. 10
6. M & Ms
7. Atlantic & Pacific
8. Fifth Avenue
9. Go into space
10. Vitamin D

Round 4

1. The Cold War
2. Alcatraz
3. 8
4. S
5. Explosion of a star
6. Canada
7. Magma
8. Apollo 11
9. Thames
10. Curse of the Black Pearl

Round 5

1. English
2. Hogwarts
3. Four or five
4. Two
5. Melon
6. Venus
7. Stone Age
8. False
9. PH 7
10. The seven seas and continents

Quiz Nine-Bonus Round Answers

1. The 50 star American Flag
2. 5
3. McCarran International Airport

Quiz 10

Round 1

1. How many time zones is the world divided into?
2. What is the capital of the Czech Republic?
3. With reference to sound, what do the letters dB stand for?
4. Which famous explorer was stabbed to death in Hawaii?
5. Which Disney character sang 'Let it Go' in the Disney movie Frozen?
6. What island is New York's Statue of Liberty located on?
7. What are igneous, sedimentary and metamorphic the three main types of?
8. How many countries border Germany?
9. Where did Moses receive the Ten Commandments?
10. What date is Earth Day celebrated annually?

Round

1. Who composed Moonlight Sonata?
2. What is the highest number on the pH scale?
3. Which Royal Navy vessel was commanded by Captain James Cook on his first voyage of discovery to Australia and New Zealand?
4. Which infamous gangster was known by the nicknames of Jackrabbit and Public Enemy No. 1?
5. Which ocean separates Africa and South America?
6. Which famous actress featured in the movies of Calamity Jane, Pillow Talk, and Young at Heart?
7. What are deciduous teeth?
8. Which Christian Feast Day is held on March 17th?
9. Which imaginary creature has the head of a man and body of a lion?
10. In which movie is the following quote used, 'What I do have is a very particular set of skills'?

Round 3

1. What nationality is soccer player Lionel Messi?
2. What is the Iditarod Race?
3. Florence Nightingale was born in Florence. True or false?
4. Are turtles reptiles or amphibians?
5. What is Prince Harry's first real name?
6. What symbol is produced on an English keyboard when the shift key and 0 are pressed together?
7. True or false: Easter has a fixed date?
8. How many events does the women's heptathlon consist of?
9. In the nursery rhyme, what was Little Jack Horner eating?
10. What is a liger?

Round 4

1. What is the fastest land animal in the world?
2. True or false: Adults blink more often than babies?
3. Complete Meatloaf's opening song lyrics: 'And I would do anything for love, I'd run right into...'?
4. If you were born on the 8th April, which star sign would you belong to?
5. In cockney rhyming slang, what is the saying 'trouble and strife' referring to?
6. What do the Roman numerals CX stand for?
7. From which country does the beer Stella Artois originate?
8. In which year did Michael Jackson release his single Thriller?
9. How many years of marriage would be celebrated by a golden anniversary?
10. What do the letters LCD stand for?

Round 5

1. What is the largest State of the USA?
2. What do dates grow on?
3. Which group had a hit with 'The Final Countdown' in 1987?
4. What is a barracuda?
5. Which animal is the emblem of Bacardi rum?
6. Which famous actor starred in the series 'The Fresh Prince of Bel-Air'?
7. Which illness is also known as the kissing disease?
8. Who had a hit with 'Firework' in 2010?
9. What is the birthstone of the star sign Aquarius?
10. What is the name given to a group of leopards?

Quiz Ten-Bonus Round Questions

1. To the nearest minute, how long does it take sunlight to travel to Earth?
2. How many tales are told in the Canterbury Tales?
3. What was John Tyler doing when he was informed that he had become US President?

Answers Quiz Ten

Round 1

1. 24
2. Prague
3. Decibels
4. Captain James Cook
5. Queen Elsa
6. Liberty Island
7. Rock
8. Nine
9. Mount Sinai
10. April 22nd

Round 2

1. Beethoven
2. pH 14
3. HMS Endeavour
4. John Dillinger
5. Atlantic Ocean
6. Doris Day
7. Primary (Baby) teeth
8. St Patrick's Day
9. Sphinx
10. Taken

Round 3

1. Argentine
2. Dog sled race
3. True
4. Reptiles
5. Henry
6. Closed bracket
7. False
8. Seven
9. Christmas pie
10. Offspring of a male lion and female tiger

Round 4

1. Cheetah
2. True
3. Hell and Back
4. Aries
5. Wife
6. 110
7. Belgium
8. 1984
9. 50
10. Liquid Crystal Display

Round 5

1. Alaska
2. Palm trees
3. Europe
4. Fish
5. Bat
6. Will Smith
7. Glandular fever
8. Katy Perry
9. Amethyst
10. A leap

Quiz Ten-Bonus Round Answers

1. 8 minutes
2. 24
3. Playing marbles

Quiz 11

Round 1

1. What colour is a New York taxi?
2. What is the abbreviated word 'fax' short for?
3. Which is heavier, gold or silver?
4. What is the biggest manmade structure on Earth?
5. Popeye has a tattoo on his arm, what is the tattoo of?
6. Where does the president of the United States of America reside?
7. What is the smallest instrument in an orchestra?
8. What colour eyes do babies initially have when they are first born?
9. Who had an 80's hit with the song 'I'm Too Sexy'?
10. What was the original name of Mickey Mouse?

Round 2

1. What do the letters SPF on sunscreen stand for?
2. Who wrote the series of 'The Famous Five' children's books?
3. Which character did Jennifer Aniston play in the sitcom 'Friends'?
4. What is the astrological sign of the star sign Cancer?
5. Who famously said 'I'm the president of the United States and I'm not going to eat any more broccoli'?
6. How many leaves does a shamrock have?
7. What is the meaning of the word 'penultimate'?
8. What language is spoken in Austria?
9. On a standard English language keyboard, what letter is located between E and T?
10. In modern days and often used through text messaging, what do the letters LOL stand for?

Round 3

1. What was the name of Barney Rubble's wife in the Flintstones?
2. Who played the role of Mary Poppins in the original film?
3. Whose treasure was buried in Treasure Island?
4. Which female character from The Thunderbirds drove a pink Rolls Royce?
5. What is the surname of the Queen of the United Kingdom and Commonwealth Realms?
6. Which chemical compound is traditionally used in Christmas crackers to make them bang?

7. What traditional New Year's Eve song begins with the lyrics, 'Should auld acquaintance be forgot'?
8. During which century did Blackbeard become famous for seafaring?
9. The Ring of Fire is located in the basin of which ocean?
10. Which celebration is less commonly known as 'the eve of All Saints' Day'?

Round 4

1. What sport is the Kieran event associated with?
2. Khartoum is the capital of which country?
3. The digestive system delivers nutrients to cells via what?
4. What is the time difference between London, UK and Sydney, Australia?
5. What is a cosmonaut?
6. Who was the first recorded European to reach the east coast of Australia?
7. Which sea does the River Rhine empty into?
8. True or False: Buzz Aldrin's mother's maiden name was Moon?
9. What is the largest species of penguin?
10. What is the chemical symbol for magnesium on the periodic table?

Round 5

1. What sports form an Olympic triathlon?
2. How many square meters are there in a hectare?
3. How many rings does Saturn have around it?
4. How many strings does a standard Spanish guitar have?
5. Which of the five senses develops first?
6. Who was the President of the US at the beginning of the 20th century?
7. What was the name of the actress that John McEnroe married?
8. In which ocean is Hawaii situated?
9. Which star sign is represented by the twins
10. How many carats are there in pure gold?

Quiz Eleven-Bonus Round Questions

1. What occupation was Murphy, famous for instigating, Murphy's Law?
2. How many voyages did Sinbad the Sailor make?
3. In which African country did Elizabeth Taylor and Richard Burton re-marry in 1975?

Answers Quiz Eleven

Round 1

1. Yellow
2. Facsimile
3. Gold
4. The Great Wall of China
5. An anchor
6. At the White House
7. Piccolo
8. Blue
9. Right Said Fred
10. Mortimer Mouse

Round 2

1. Sun Protection Factor
2. Enid Blyton
3. Rachel Green
4. The crab
5. George W Bush
6. Three
7. The second last
8. German
9. R
10. Laugh out loud

Round 3

1. Betty Rubble
2. Julie Andrews
3. Captain Flint's
4. Lady Penelope
5. Windsor
6. Silver fulminate
7. Auld Lang Syne
8. 18th century
9. Pacific Ocean
10. Halloween

Round 4

1. Cycling
2. Sudan
3. The bloodstream
4. 9 hours
5. Russian space traveller
6. Captain James Cook
7. North Sea
8. True
9. Emperor penguin
10. Mg

Round 5

1. Swimming, running, cycling
2. 10000
3. Seven main ring groups
4. Six
5. Smell
6. William McKinley
7. Tatum O'Neal
8. Pacific Ocean
9. Gemini
10. Twenty four

Quiz Eleven-Bonus Round Answers

1. Lifeguard
2. Seven
3. Botswana

Quiz 12

Round 1

1. Which acid can be found in vinegar?
2. What is the name of the man who invented the computer mouse?
3. Which South American country was named after the Italian city of Venice?
4. In which country were the 2008 Olympic Games held?
5. What was the name of Connie Booth's character in the sitcom 'Fawlty Towers'?
6. What type of food is manchego?
7. In 1992, who did the Princess Royal (Anne) marry?
8. What is the name of the boy in the Jungle Book?
9. Which group of Europeans are believed to have first entered America?
10. Which celebrity is rapper Jay-Z married to?

Round 2

1. What is a Macaw a type of?
2. In the cartoon, what is the name of the bird that Sylvester chases?
3. Who plays King Arthur in Monty Python and The Holy Grail?
4. Which element is coal mainly composed of?
5. What do the rings on the Olympic Games symbol represent?
6. In the film 'Meet the Parents' who plays the character Greg?
7. Which jubilee did Queen Elizabeth II celebrate in 2012?
8. Which dish are battered deep-fried squid rings known as?
9. In the film 'Nanny McPhee', who played the role of Nanny McPhee?
10. What part of a horse would you examine to tell its age?

Round 3

1. Who wrote the famous musical entitled 'Oliver'?
2. What is the biggest spider in the world?
3. Which fairy tale character was cursed to sleep for 100 years?
4. In which country was the first car radio made?
5. Which sport is known as the Sport of Kings?
6. How many keys does a standard full size piano have?
7. Which rock band did Brian May belong to?
8. Which musical instrument is James Galway famous for playing?
9. Which sport is mintonette now known as?
10. Where was the first nuclear reactor built?

Round 4

1. Which brewery invented the widget for the beer can?
2. What is the only mammal that is able to kneel on all fours?
3. Which country is Santiago the capital of?
4. Which is the largest species of crocodile?
5. Where did King Arthur hold court?
6. Which country was Arnold Schwarzenegger born in?
7. Which nuts are used to make marzipan?
8. What is the name of Washington's active stratovolcano?
9. In which country were 'The Lord of the Rings' movies filmed?
10. Which character did Clark Gable play in Gone with the Wind?

Round 5

1. Which word can come before: moon, house and time?
2. Which Roman numerals represent the number 40?
3. How many hours are there in one full week?
4. Which AFL team has the most members? (as of 2019)
5. What were the Christian names of the explorers Burke and Wills?
6. Who was the leading actor in the Australian series Matlock Police?
7. Which actor starred in Gangs of New York and Lincoln?
8. What was the name of Moses' brother
9. Who sang the 2015 hit song 'All About That Bass'?
10. What is an obtuse angle?

Quiz Twelve-Bonus Round Questions

1. What is Fidel Castro's first name?
2. What does a cordwainer make?
3. What was the name of the first waterproof watch made by Rolex?

Answers Quiz Twelve

Round 1

1. Acetic acid
2. Doug Englebart
3. Venezuela
4. China (Beijing)
5. Polly
6. Cheese
7. Timothy Lawrence
8. Mowgli
9. The Vikings
10. Beyoncé

Round 2

1. A parrot (bird)
2. Tweety Pie
3. Graham Chapman
4. Carbon
5. The continents
6. Ben Stiller
7. Diamond
8. Calamari
9. Emma Thompson
10. The teeth

Round 3

1. Lionel Bart
2. Goliath birdeater
3. Sleeping Beauty
4. USA
5. Horse racing
6. Eighty eight
7. Queen
8. Flute
9. Volleyball
10. USA

Round 4

1. Guinness
2. Elephant
3. Chile
4. Saltwater
5. Camelot
6. Austria
7. Almonds
8. Mt St Helens
9. New Zealand
10. Rhett Butler

Round 5

1. Full
2. XL
3. 168
4. Richmond
5. Robert, William
6. Michael Pate
7. Daniel Day Lewis
8. Aaron
9. Meghan Trainor
10. An angle greater than 90 degrees but less than 180 degrees

Quiz Twelve-Bonus Round Answers

1. Ruz
2. Shoes
3. Oyster

Quiz 13

Round 1

1. Which US President gave the famous Gettysburg Address Speech?
2. Which notorious 18th Century British pirate wore a beard and became famous for operating around the West Indies and the east coasts of the American colonies?
3. During which war did Florence Nightingale attend to wounded soldiers?
4. What was the name of the legendary sword of King Arthur?
5. Which country was General Franco a dictator of?
6. What famous wall, built by a Roman Emperor, lies between Scotland and England?
7. During which year did Fidel Castro gain power over Cuba?
8. What is the name of the city where John F. Kennedy was assassinated?
9. Which war first introduced the use of tanks?
10. Since retiring from service, where is the QE2 docked on a permanent basis?

Round 2

1. Which famous artist painted the ceiling of the Sistine Chapel?
2. What was the Flying Scotsman?
3. In which country was the Statue of Zeus located?
4. Which British King of the 20ᵗʰ Century had a stutter?
5. Who became Prime Minister of Australia in 1983?
6. In Australian music, who was known as The Wild One?
7. Which country did Iraq invade in 1990?
8. What was the name of the first woman to fly solo across the Atlantic?
9. What is the name given to the Pirate's flag that bears the skull and cross bones?
10. In 1999, which country voted to keep the Queen?

Round 3

1. Who was the President of America before Barack Obama?
2. What did Guy Fawkes attempt to blow up?
3. Which SANFL club has won 15 Premierships? (as of 2019)
4. Which Australian Prime Minister was known as The Little Digger?
5. How many Brownlow Medals did Bob Skilton win?
6. Which two countries fought during the Falklands War?
7. Who was the first person to reach the South Pole?
8. Who succeeded Franklin D Roosevelt as President?
9. Who became Prime Minister of the United Kingdom in 2010?
10. What was the largest of the dinosaurs?

Round 4

1. Which nation invented fireworks?
2. How many times was Winston Churchill Prime Minister over the United Kingdom?
3. Which nation attacked a US Navy base at Pearl Harbour in December 1941?
4. Who stepped onto the moon shortly after Neil Armstrong?
5. What is the name of Lord Nelson's flagship?
6. What type of vehicle is the Immelmann turn associated with?
7. Which popular European sport was pioneered by Scandinavian immigrants in Australia?
8. What is the larynx better known as?
9. The gooney bird is better known as what?
10. Why has Oslo donated a Christmas tree to Trafalgar Square, London since 1947?

Round 5

1. Which Russian spy sought political asylum in Australia in 1954?
2. Who wrote the lyrics to the song The Boxer?
3. What does a protractor measure?
4. Jan Davis and Mark Lee were the first married couple to do what?
5. Which part of the body contains the labyrinth?
6. In which country is the most easternmost point of South America?
7. What do the initials GMT stand for?
8. What did Louis Cartier invent in 1904?
9. Which Australian racetrack hosts the WS Cox Plate every year?
10. Who played Don Bradman in the TV mini-series Bodyline?

Quiz Thirteen-Bonus Round Questions

1. How many Gold Logies did Graham Kennedy win?
2. During which year did the London Underground first open?
3. What was the name of Buddha's son?

Answers Quiz Thirteen

Round 1

1. Abraham Lincoln
2. Blackbeard
3. The Crimean War
4. Excalibur
5. Spain
6. Hadrian's Wall
7. 1959
8. Dallas, Texas
9. World War I
10. Dubai

Round 2

1. Michelangelo
2. A train
3. Greece
4. King George VI
5. Bob Hawke
6. Johnny O'Keefe
7. Kuwait
8. Amelia Earhart
9. Jolly Roger
10. Australia

Round 3

1. George W Bush
2. Houses of Parliament
3. Sturt
4. Billy Hughes
5. Three
6. Great Britain, Argentina
7. Roald Amundsen
8. Harry S Truman
9. David Cameron
10. Argentinosaurus huinculensis

Round 4

1. China
2. Twice
3. Japan
4. Buzz Aldrin
5. HMS Victory
6. Aircraft
7. Snow ski-ing
8. Voice box
9. Albatross
10. Gratitude for support in WWII

Round 5

1. Vladimir Petrov
2. Paul Simon
3. Geometric angles
4. Fly in space
5. Ear
6. Brazil
7. Greenwich Mean Time
8. Wristwatch
9. Moonee Valley
10. Gary Sweet

Quiz Thirteen- Bonus Round Answers

1. 5
2. 1863
3. Rahula

Quiz 14

Round 1

1. What is the highest straight flush in a game of poker?
2. Hombro is Spanish for which part of the body?
3. An agal is worn on which part of the body?
4. Who played the title role in the 1996 film 'The English Patient'?
5. Which singer got her hair caught in the blades of a fan as she was performing in concert in Montreal in July 2013?
6. The 1992 film 'Wayne's World' was a spin-off of a sketch from which US television show?
7. In the theatre, topophobia is commonly known as what?
8. Comedian Larry David starred in the US television show 'Curb Your 'what'?
9. Spell the human lung condition pleurisy.
10. What is the capital of Kuwait?

Round 2

1. 'Songs My Mother Taught Me' is a 1995 autobiography by which US actor?
2. In the George Orwell novel 'Animal Farm', who is the owner of Pinchfield Farm?
3. Which country is bordered by the Gaza Strip, Israel, Libya and Sudan?
4. What is the name of the family's pet goldfish in the US television cartoon series 'American Dad'?
5. In the US television series, what type of car did Starsky and Hutch drive?
6. In which country is the River Darling?
7. What is the name of the Jack Russell dog in the US television series 'Frasier'?
8. Which British singer released a 1975 album entitled 'Rock of the Westies'?
9. Which is the fifth largest country in the world by area?
10. Helena is the capital of which US state?

Round 3

1. What is the first name of the Australian Prime Minister's wife? (as of 2019)
2. VA is the abbreviation of which US state?
3. In October 1977 three members of which US rock band died in a plane crash in Mississippi, three days after the release of their album 'Street Survivors'?
4. Suva is the capital of which South Pacific island?
5. A bammy is a flatbread originating in which country?
6. On a regular clock face which number lies opposite 2?
7. Which US mobster is quoted as saying 'Capitalism is the legitimate racket of the ruling class'?
8. Who plays Calvin J Candie in the 2012 film 'Django Unchained'?
9. What beer is marketed as the king of beers?
10. Who was born Leslie Townes Hope?

Round 4

1. How is the number 5 written in Roman numerals?
2. In American football, how many points is a touchdown worth?
3. Which Quentin Tarantino movie won the "Best Picture" or prestigious Palme d'Or at the Cannes Film Festival in 1994?
4. What is a baby seal called?
5. Who were the backing group for Bill Hailey?
6. In which year was the wedding of Prince Charles and Lady Diana Spencer?
7. Which King's defeat ended the War of the Roses?
8. Which Bulgarian sculptor is famous for wrapping things up?
9. What nationality was Greg Rusedski before he became a British tennis star?
10. If New Year's Day is the first day of the year, what number is Christmas Day?

Round 5

1. In which country was Che Guevara born?
2. Which African country is directly north of Namibia
3. True or False? Nicole Kidman was born in Hawaii.
4. In which city is the Australian Open tennis tournament held annually?
5. Which Australian won the 1973 Nobel Prize for literature?
6. The Great Barrier Reef is located in which sea?
7. Give the name of the largest desert in Australia - it spans Western and South Australia?
8. Which American television sitcom follows the lives of roommates Caroline and Max?
9. How many years are celebrated in a traditional 'Pearl Wedding Anniversary'?
10. Which shirt number would you associate with ice hockey legend Wayne Gretzky?

Quiz Fourteen-Bonus Round Questions

1. Bati beer is brewed in which African country?
2. Where is Torshavn the largest city?
3. What military device did the father of Alfred Nobel invent?

Answers Quiz Fourteen

Round 1

1. Royal Flush
2. Shoulder
3. Head
4. Ralph Fiennes
5. Beyoncé
6. Saturday Night Live
7. Stage fright
8. Enthusiasm
9. Pleurisy
10. Kuwait City

Round 2

1. Marlon Brando
2. Mr Frederick
3. Egypt
4. Klaus Heissler
5. Gran Torino
6. Australia
7. Eddie
8. Elton John
9. Brazil
10. Montana

Round 3

1. Jenny
2. Virginia
3. Lynryd Skynyrd
4. Fiji
5. Jamaica
6. 8
7. Al Capone
8. Leonardo DiCaprio
9. Budweiser
10. Bob Hope

Round 4

1. V
2. 6
3. Pulp Fiction
4. A pup
5. The Comets
6. 1981
7. Richard III
8. Christo
9. Canadian
10. 359th

Round 5

1. Argentina
2. Angola
3. True
4. Melbourne
5. Patrick White
6. Coral Sea
7. Great Victoria Desert
8. 2 Broke Girls
9. 30
10. 99

Quiz Fourteen-Bonus Round Answers

1. Ethiopia
2. Faroe islands
3. Naval mine

Quiz 15

Round 1

1. Scrumpy is a type of which alcoholic drink?
2. Which late singer was known as the 'Electric Poet'?
3. An atoll is formed by which natural substance?
4. Port-of-Spain is the capital of which Caribbean republic?
5. Which famous British author used the pen name Mary Westmacott?
6. What are the names of Peter Rabbit's sisters in 'The Tale of Peter Rabbit' by Beatrix Potter?
7. What are the name of the veins on each side of the neck which drain blood from the head and neck to larger veins passing to the heart?
8. Who wrote the novel 'The Invisible Man', published in 1897?
9. Mount Chimborazo is in which South American country?
10. In sport, what does IOC stand for?

Round 2

1. What is the basic monetary unit of Israel?
2. Demophobia is the irrational fear of what?
3. A piculet is which type of creature?
4. Who directed the 1987 film 'Full Metal Jacket'?
5. In which European country is Lake Ree?
6. The magazine Marie Claire was first published in 1937 in which country?
7. Haneda Airport is in which Asian country?
8. In which part of the human body is the organ of Corti?
9. Who plays Susan Delfino in the US TV series Desperate Housewives?
10. The Winter War from 1939 – 1940 was a military conflict between Russia (Soviet Union) and which other country?

Round 3

1. A curassow is what type of creature?
2. Which of Henry VIII's wives was known as the Flanders Mare?
3. A philogynist likes or admires who?
4. What colour are the stars on the national flag of China?
5. Where on a horse's body is the frog?
6. What was the name of the camp which was set up in Chile when 30 miners were trapped underground?
7. The litas was the basic monetary unit of which country?
8. Which vegetable was the first to be canned?
9. Which US state is known as the 'Beef State'?
10. Anime is film animation originating in which country?

Round 4

1. In computers, the X-Y Position Indicator for a Display System is now known as what?
2. Which country has the internet domain '.ch'?
3. Adelost cheese is made in which European country?
4. Which former US boxer is referred to as the 'Poet laureate of boxing'?
5. From which decade of the 20th Century did Wales have a capital city?
6. A Spinone is what type of animal?
7. How many stones are used in a game of curling?
8. Which letter is furthest to the right on a top letter row on a computer keyboard?
9. Which Asian country is known as the 'Land of Smiles'?
10. In private healthcare what does BUPA stand for?

Round 5

1. What is the surname of Buffy, the Vampire Slayer, in the US television series?
2. What is the US state capital of Florida?
3. Toucher, Narrow and Bias are all terms used in which sport?
4. In 2002 Steve Fossett became the first solo person to circumnavigate the world non-stop and single-handed in what?
5. What is the title of The Beatles first feature film, released in 1964?
6. Vestiphobia is the irrational fear of which items?
7. Which country hosted the 1998 Winter Olympic Games?
8. Which island is divided among Brunei, Malaysia and Indonesia?
9. Arancione is Italian for which colour?
10. What type of foodstuff is a cascabel?

Quiz Fifteen-Bonus Round Questions

1. The Greek national anthem has a total of how many verses (or stanzas)?
2. Which band's 2007 album is entitled 'Send Away the Tigers'?
3. The Pantheon was built for which Roman Emperor?

Answers Quiz Fifteen

Round 1

1. Cider
2. Jim Morrison
3. Coral
4. Trinidad & Tobago
5. Agatha Christie
6. Flopsy, Mopsy, Cottontail
7. Jugular
8. H.G.Wells
9. Ecuador
10. International Olympic Committee

Round 2

1. Shekel
2. Crowds
3. Birds
4. Stanley Kubrick
5. Ireland
6. France
7. Japan
8. Ear (cochlea)
9. Teri Hatcher
10. Finland

Round 3

1. Bird
2. Anne of Cleves
3. Women
4. Yellow
5. Hoof
6. Camp Hope
7. Lithuania
8. Peas
9. Nebraska
10. Japan

Round 4

1. Cursor
2. Switzerland
3. Sweden
4. Floyd Mayweather Snr
5. 1950s
6. Dog
7. 16
8. P
9. Thailand
10. British United Provident Association

Round 5

1. Summers
2. Tallahassee
3. Lawn bowls
4. Hot air balloon
5. A Hard Day's Night
6. Clothes
7. Japan
8. Borneo
9. Orange
10. Chilli pepper

Quiz Fifteen-Bonus Round Answers

1. 158
2. Manic Street Preachers
3. Hadrian

Quiz 16

Round 1

1. The stirrup bone is in the human what?
2. Brioche is a French type of what?
3. The global spate of clown hoaxers in 2016 was said to be a PR stunt organized for the remake of which film?
4. Among other works, Dutch artist M C Escher is especially famous for pictures of impossible what?
5. What three letter prefix makes new words when added to: Due; Urban, Marine, Traction, and Way?
6. The word Muscovite refers to what?
7. Based on the German legend of Dr Faustus, a Faustian Bargain is alternatively called a what?
8. What file extension abbreviation is traditionally used for a 'read-only' Adobe Acrobat documents?
9. Who in 2016 became the first singer-songwriter to be awarded a Nobel Prize for Literature?
10. What is the popular annual Hindu Festival of Lights called?

Round 2

1. What instrument used by Marilyn Monroe in Some Like It Hot was patented in Hawaii in 1917?
2. What can be worn in the NATO phonetic alphabet, derived from which letter?
3. A healthy/normal human adult blood pressure reading is considered to be roughly what two figures?
4. Which of these is not a major export of Cuba: Sugar; Tobacco; Citrus fruit; or Lamb?
5. Chuck Taylor popularized what 1908-founded US shoe corporation, whose logo is a single circled star?
6. 'Light amplification by stimulated emission of radiation' is better known as what, first demonstrated in 1960?
7. The Equator lies at how many degrees latitude?
8. The Iliad and Odyssey are classical Greek epic poems about the Trojan War written by whom?
9. What modern entertainment was originally an ancient religious practice: Juggling; Ventriloquism; Sword-swallowing; or Tap dancing?
10. Cyclops is an ancient Greek mythological giant with one what?

Round 3

1. A cloven foot (of cows, sheep, goats, etc.) has how many toes or grounded hoof parts?
2. The first famously cloned sheep of 1996, was named what?

3. Snatch, Clean, and Jerk feature in which sport?
4. What are the markings on a cricket pitch are called?
5. The Alsatian dog name refers to a region of which modern country?
6. Cyclamen is a group term referring to small what?
7. Chicano refers to mixed American and which other ethnicity?
8. A theodolite is traditionally used by whom?
9. Roughly how many planet Earths would fit into the Sun? 100; 1,000; 10,000; or 1 million?
10. The wine grape Shiraz (Syrah) is widely said to originate from which nation's city of Shiraz?

Round 4

1. Put the EBay logo letters in correct colour order.
2. Hanukkah is a November/December eight-day festival of which religion?
3. Appalachia is a region associated with mountainous countryside in which country?
4. Perpendicular refers to an angle of how many degrees?
5. In tennis a legal serve which cannot be reached by the opponent is called what?
6. What is the mown grass between the tees and holes on a golf course called?
7. Who was the first actor to refuse an Oscar (Academy Award) for Best Actor?
8. A traditional Easter pageant dramatic presentation of the end of Christ's life is also called a (What?) Play?
9. What was the previous brand-name of the Nissan automotive corporation?
10. Who was elected the President of France in 2012?

Round 5

1. The mariachi musical style/band belongs to which country?
2. What Latin term refers to a writer or composer's 'great work'?
3. What is the international dialling code for Australia?
4. How many eighths are in one-and-three-quarters?
5. What is the main metallic element in the core of the moon?
6. Anachronistic means from another what?
7. Cape Verde was until independence a territory of which European country?
8. Erected in 1989, what large geometric glass structure serves as the main entrance to the Louvre Museum in Paris?
9. What significant territory did President Richard Nixon call by telephone on 20 July 1969?
10. What creature is on the mission insignia or badge of the first moon landing, Apollo 11?

Answers Quiz Sixteen

Round 1

1. Ear
2. Bread
3. IT
4. Staircases
5. Sub
6. Citizen of Moscow
7. A deal with the devil
8. PDF
9. Bob Dylan
10. Diwali

Round 2

1. Ukulele
2. Uniform
3. 120/80
4. Lamb
5. Converse
6. Laser
7. 0 degrees
8. Homer
9. Ventriloquism
10. Eye

Round 3

1. Two
2. Dolly
3. Weightlifting
4. Creases
5. France
6. Flowering plants
7. Mexican
8. Surveyor
9. One million
10. Iran

Round 4

1. Red, blue, yellow green
2. Judaism
3. USA
4. 90
5. An ace
6. Fairway
7. George C Scott
8. Passion
9. Datsun
10. Francois Hollande

Round 5

1. Mexico
2. Magnum Opus
3. 61
4. 14
5. Iron
6. Time
7. Portugal
8. Pyramid
9. The moon
10. Eagle

Quiz Sixteen-Bonus Round Questions

1. Who was the last English monarch to win the throne on the battlefield?
2. In which English town was navigator Matthew Flinders born?
3. Cycling legend, Sir Hubert Opperman served as Australia's ambassador to which country?

Quiz Sixteen-Bonus Round Answers

1. Henry VII
2. Donington
3. Malta

Quiz 17

Round 1

1. What major international leader was in 2010 officially given ranked status as a Hells Angel by his nation's 'high council' of bikers?
2. What is Bratwurst made mainly out of?
3. Which animal features on India's national emblem?
4. What was the name of the African-American revolutionary organization founded in the US in 1966 by Huey Newton and Bobby Seale?
5. Who was the founder of Wikileaks?
6. To which country did Amazon move its European HQ in 2006?
7. What model pioneered personal computing in the 1980s?
8. Name the passenger vehicle that had 36 fatalities on 6 May 1937 at New Jersey US?
9. Spell the city name: Phnom Penh.
10. Earl Scruggs pioneered and was master of the three-fingered technique for playing what instrument?

Round 2

1. Facebook announced the acquisition of what major photo app company in April 2012?
2. What does perfunctory mean?
3. What two countries did the Titanic visit after leaving Southampton on its doomed maiden voyage?
4. What African country experienced a 2012 rebellion by Tuareg fighters?
5. Which major social networking corporation grew from a branded messaging project at podcasting site Odeo?
6. Who succeeded Joseph Stalin as leader of the Soviet Union?
7. Who was Australian Prime Minister in the 1950s?
8. Which Greek hero killed the 'half-man/half-bull' Minotaur?
9. Which country has the longest national highway in the world?
10. What is the only country whose homeland spans Africa and Asia?

Round 3

1. What traditionally mysterious, increasingly transparent organization is casually referred to as 'The Craft'?
2. Coptic refers to a sect of what religious order?
3. Roughly how long did the Pony Express service operate in the USA?
4. What does 'swaddling' mean?
5. Who in the 1970s was the first big sports superstar endorsee of the Fila brand?

6. Who was the intruder who woke and spoke to Elizabeth II in her bedroom in Buckingham Palace in 1982
7. What country inspired the term banana republic?
8. Which letter is represented by a single dot in Morse code?
9. How many X chromosomes do women have?
10. The acronym STEM in education refers to a set of what four technical subjects?

Round 4

1. Which country is the natural habitat of the emu?
2. Which city is the largest port in Germany?
3. Which African city means 'the place of combat'?
4. Which state borders California to the north?
5. Who is the druid in the Asterix books?
6. What is the name of the recreated theatre from Shakespeare's time in London?
7. Who was caught red-handed trying to blow up parliament in 1605?
8. What title was given to the rulers of Ancient Egypt?
9. Air Force One is a plane used by the holder of what position?
10. What sort of animal is Basil Brush?

Round 5

1. In which town do the Flintstones live?
2. What is the name of Shrek's wife?
3. What is the name of the hero in The Lion King?
4. In netball, for what does WA stand?
5. How many pieces does a player have in Ludo?
6. What kind of animal is Beatrix Potter's Mrs Tiggy-Winkle?
7. Which actress was Ronald Reagan's first wife?
8. Who wrote the book The Natural?
9. At which Stalag were Hogan's Heroes stationed?
10. What were discovered by a shepherd in Jordan in 1947?

Quiz Seventeen-Bonus Round Questions

1. Who was awarded the first Best Actress Academy Award in 1929?
2. What was the first event decided at the 1896 Olympic Games?
3. How many children did actress Jayne Mansfield have?

Answers Quiz Seventeen

Round 1

1. Vladimir Putin
2. Meat
3. Lion
4. Black Panther Party
5. Julian Assange
6. Luxembourg
7. Commodore 64
8. Hindenburg
9. Phnom Penh
10. Banjo

Round 2

1. Instagram
2. Careless
3. France & Ireland
4. Mali
5. Twitter
6. Nikita Khrushchev
7. Robert Menzies
8. Theseus
9. Australia Highway 1
10. Egypt

Round 3

1. Freemasonry
2. Christianity
3. One year
4. Wrapping in cloth
5. Bjorn Borg
6. Michael Fagan
7. Honduras
8. E
9. 2
10. Science, Technology Engineering, Maths

Round 4

1. Australia
2. Hamburg
3. Cairo
4. Oregon
5. Getafix
6. The Globe
7. Guy Fawkes
8. Pharaohs
9. President of USA
10. Fox

Round 5

1. Bedrock
2. Princess Fiona
3. Simba
4. Wing attack
5. Four
6. Hedgehog
7. Jane Wyman
8. Bernard Malamud
9. Stalag 13
10. Dead Sea Scrolls

Quiz Seventeen-Bonus Round Answers

1. Janet Gaynor
2. Triple jump
3. Five

Quiz 18

Round 1

1. Vodka, Galliano and orange juice are used to make which classic cocktail?
2. On TV, who did the character Lurch work for?
3. Which children's classic book was written by Anna Sewell?
4. How many arms/tentacles/limbs does a squid have?
5. Which reggae singing star died 11th May 1981?
6. In what year was Prince Andrew born?
7. If cats are feline, what are sheep?
8. In the song, Heartbreak Hotel is on which street?
9. Characters Charlie Allnut and Rosie Sayer appeared in which classic 1951 movie?
10. What is the policeman's name in Noddy stories?

Round 2

1. What is the word used to describe an animal/plant that is both male and female?
2. Which is the financial centre and main city of Switzerland?
3. For which fruit is the US state of Georgia famous?
4. In the 1963 film The Great Escape, what names were given to the three tunnels?
5. What does a numismatist study or collect?
6. Who captained Jules Verne's submarine Nautilus?
7. Which guitarist is known as Slowhand?
8. The llama belongs to the family of animals commonly called what?
9. The Sheffield Shield is competed for in which sport?
10. What is an infant whale commonly called?

Round 3

1. In which film did Roger Moore first play James Bond?
2. Which 17th century explorer was buried with a pipe and a box of tobacco?
3. Which Latin term, usually applied to legal evidence, means 'at first sight'?
4. What was the character name of TV's 'The Saint'?
5. Who composed The Wedding March?
6. What is the alternative common name for a Black Leopard?
7. In which bay is Alcatraz?
8. What do the British call the vegetables that Australians call zucchini?
9. In which Dickens novel was Miss Havisham jilted on her wedding day?
10. How have vegetables been cut which are served Julienne?

Round 4

1. Which mountain overlooks Rio de Janeiro and its harbour?
2. In Roman mythology, Neptune is the equivalent to which Greek god?
3. What is the only English language single word anagram of the word crouton?
4. Which TV character said, 'Live long and prosper'?
5. What make of car was the time-machine in the film Back to the Future?
6. How old is a horse when it changes from a filly to a mare?
7. What is Canada's national animal?
8. What is the colour of the bull of an archery target?
9. Which musical featured the song They Called the Wind Mariah?
10. In which war was the Battle of Bunker Hill fought?

Round 5

1. What does the phrase 'Alea iacta est' translate to in English?
2. Royal Gala is a variety of which fruit?
3. Who wrote the 1869 novel 'War and Peace'?
4. In which part of the human body are the metatarsus bones?
5. Guadalupe Island, in the Pacific Ocean, belongs to which country?
6. On which island was Napoleon Bonaparte born in 1769?
7. From which country did Russia finally withdraw its troops in 1989, after an unsuccessful campaign that lasted nearly ten years?
8. In September 1978, which Pope died after only 33 days of Papacy?
9. Which British singer entered The Guinness Book of Records in 2005, after selling 1.6 million concert tickets in one day?
10. David McConnell was the founder of which cosmetics company in 1886?

Quiz Eighteen-Bonus Round Questions

1. The Admiralty Islands in the Pacific Ocean belong to which country?
2. In what year did trainer Bart Cummings enter his first Melbourne Cup?
3. In the film series, how many children did Ma and Pa Kettle have?

Answers Quiz Eighteen

Round 1

1. Harvey Wallbanger
2. Addams Family
3. Black Beauty
4. Ten
5. Bob Marley
6. 1960
7. Ovine
8. Lonely Street
9. The African Queen
10. PC Plod

Round 2

1. Hermaphrodite
2. Zurich
3. Peach
4. Tom, Dick, Harry
5. Coins
6. Captain Nemo
7. Eric Clapton
8. Camels
9. Cricket
10. Calf

Round 3

1. Live and Let Die
2. Sir Walter Raleigh
3. Prima Facie
4. Simon Templar
5. Felix Mendelssohn
6. Panther
7. San Francisco Bay
8. Courgette
9. Great Expectations
10. Thin strips

Round 4

1. Sugar Loaf
2. Poseidon
3. Contour
4. Mr Spock
5. De Lorean
6. Four years
7. Beaver
8. Gold
9. Paint Your Wagon
10. American War of Independence

Round 5

1. The die has been cast
2. Apple
3. Leo Tolstoy
4. Foot
5. Mexico
6. Corsica
7. Afghanistan
8. Pope John Paul I
9. Robbie Williams
10. Avon

Quiz Eighteen-Bonus Round Answers

1. Papua New Guinea
2. 1958
3. 15

Quiz 19

Round 1

1. Amnesty International was founded in which year?
2. What is a female hippopotamus called?
3. Which is the smallest state by area in the US?
4. Relating to glue, what does PVA stand for?
5. What was the name of the cross-eyed lion in the TV series 'Daktari'?
6. Who played painter Paul Gauguin in the 1956 film 'Lust for Life'?
7. Who played Jodie Foster's lawyer, Kathryn Murphy, in the 1988 film 'The Accused'?
8. Which is the only US state to have only one syllable in its name?
9. What is the title of the 2000 film in which Bruce Willis plays a security guard who is the sole survivor of a train crash?
10. Pouchong tea is traditionally scented with the leaves of which flower?

Round 2

1. In the Harry Potter series of books what is the name of the Charms Master at Hogwarts School?
2. The martial art vovinam originated in which country?
3. Who was the only US President not to live at the White House?
4. What was the name of the backing group of British singer Gerry Marsden?
5. The 'Autobots' and the 'Decepticons' are the main factions of which toy line?
6. Who broke boxer Muhammad Ali's jaw in a boxing match in March 1973?
7. Roman Emperor Gaius Julius Caesar Augustus Germanicus is better known by what name?
8. The River Danube empties into which body of water?
9. The ruins of Troy are in which modern-day country?
10. 'Quicksilver' is another name for which metallic element?

Round 3

1. Which American football player was nicknamed 'The Juice'?
2. Rosalynn Smith is married to which former US President?
3. Which four letter word beginning with 'E' is a malicious grudging or ill will?
4. Which number is the title of singer Beyoncé's 2011 album?
5. What is the name of the headquarters of the US Department of Defense, located in Arlington County, Virginia?

6. What are the bars or wire rods called which connect the hub of a wheel to its rim?
7. Which European city hosted the first Olympic Games in which women were allowed to participate?
8. Which US state is known as The Land of Enchantment?
9. What is the title of the 2010 film based on the memoir of real-life canyoneer Aran Ralston, who became trapped by a boulder in an isolated canyon in Utah in April 2003?
10. Who wrote the children's story 'The Emperor's New Clothes'?

Round 4

1. The resort town of Whistler is in which Canadian province?
2. Mary Berry and Paul Hollywood are two judges on which UK television cookery show?
3. In the children's TV series, what is the name of Bob the Builder's cat?
4. What is the US state capital of Oklahoma?
5. Mark Zuckerberg and Eduardo Savarin are two of the creators of which social networking service, launched in February 2004?
6. What was the title of the book to first feature serial killer Hannibal Lector?
7. A pontil is a metal rod used in the process of what?
8. What is the second largest emirate of the Unites Arab Emirates?
9. A labeorphilist collects what type of bottles?
10. Governor Ratcliffe, Nakoma and Grandmother Willow are all characters in which Disney film?

Round 5

1. The Bay of Fundy, which has the highest tides in the world, is mainly in which country?
2. Who played the role of Darryl Kerrigan in the movie, 'The Castle'?
3. Who played Mr Brown in the 1991 film 'Reservoir Dogs'?
4. What is the name of the Tropic which lies approximately 23.5 degrees south of the Equator and runs through Australia, Chile, Brazil and South Africa?
5. Which English singer commissioned a painting of the cartoon character SpongeBob Squarepants for his house in 2008?
6. Silent film star Charlie Chaplin was born in which European city?
7. Originating in the Philippines, what is a bolo?
8. Splenitis is the inflammation of which part of the body?
9. Founded by Robert Baden Powell, what is the motto of the Boy Scouts?
10. Which English football club won the 2000 FA Cup?

Answers Quiz Nineteen

Round 1

1. 1961
2. Cow
3. Rhode Island
4. Polyvinyl Acetate
5. Clarence
6. Anthony Quinn
7. Kelly McGillis
8. Maine
9. Unbreakable
10. Rose

Round 2

1. Filius Flitwick
2. Vietnam
3. George Washington
4. The Pacemakers
5. Transformers
6. Ken Norton
7. Caligula
8. Black Sea
9. Turkey
10. Mercury

Round 3

1. OJ Simpson
2. Jimmy Carter
3. Envy
4. 4
5. The Pentagon
6. Spokes
7. Paris 1900
8. New Mexico
9. 127 hours
10. Hans Christian Anderson

Round 4

1. British Columbia
2. Great British Bake Off
3. Pilchard
4. Oklahoma City
5. Facebook
6. Red Dragon
7. Glass blowing
8. Dubai
9. Beer bottles
10. Pocahontas

Round 5

1. Canada
2. Michael Caton
3. Quentin Tarantino
4. Tropic of Capricorn
5. Liam Gallagher
6. London
7. Knife/machete
8. Spleen
9. Be prepared
10. Chelsea

Quiz Nineteen-Bonus Round Questions

1. Who is Andreas Cornelius van Kujik better known as?
2. What is the name of the official Scottish residence of the British monarch?
3. How many years did it take to decriminalise homosexuality in all the Australian states and territories?

Quiz Nineteen-Bonus Round Answers

1. Colonel Tom Parker (Elvis Presley's manager)
2. The Palace of Holy Roodhouse
3. 22 years (1975-1997)

Quiz 20

Round 1

1. What is the other name for Wildebeest?
2. Which actor appeared in Papillion and The Great Escape and died in 1980?
3. The volcano Hekla is on which island?
4. Who became US President in 1913?
5. British singer Stuart Goddard is better known by what name?
6. Who was the first British monarch to travel by train?
7. Which playing card is known as 'Lancelot'?
8. In the Christian calendar, what does AD stand for?
9. In mathematics, how many sides does a rhombus have?
10. The city of Buffalo lies on which North American Great Lake?

Round 2

1. What is the lowest denomination Euro banknote?
2. Dermatology is the study of which part of the human body?
3. Who developed bifocal spectacles in 1784?
4. Who wrote the 'Winnie the Pooh' books?
5. In the nursery rhyme, who 'Kissed the girls and made them cry'?
6. Which chemical compound has the molecular formula H_2O_2?
7. What is the first name of World Champion Formula One racing driver Vettel?
8. Free Byrd is a tribute band to which US band?
9. What is the official language of Barbados?
10. Which US singer married Debbie Reynolds, Elizabeth Taylor and Connie Stevens?

Round 3

1. Which is the only letter of the alphabet that does not appear in the name of any of the states of America?
2. Who became the first female Prime Minister of Israel, in 1969?
3. Which word starting with I is a painting of a holy figure used as an aid to devotion, and a graphic representation on a computer?
4. In the human body, toxaemia is more commonly known by what name?
5. Which mountain is known as 'The White Spider'?
6. What is the first name of Wimbledon tennis champion Federer?
7. Which 'A' word means in the open air?
8. Which late actor played Albus Dumbledore in the first two Harry Potter films?
9. In the Star Wars series of films what is the name of the slug-like alien who had a bounty on Han Solo, who owed him money for dumping an illegal cargo?
10. What do the letters ASX stand for?

Round 4

1. Who was British Prime Minister in 1994?
2. In April 1993, the World Health Organisation declared which disease 'A global health emergency'?
3. In mathematics, how many degrees are in a straight angle?
4. Who wrote the 1898 book 'The War of the Worlds'?
5. The headquarters of the International Ice Hockey Federation is in which European city?
6. What is the only city in the US not technically located in a state?
7. In November 1990, Mary Robinson defeated Brian Lenihan to become the first female President of which country?
8. The New York Rangers represent the city in which sport?
9. 'Where Everybody Knows Your Name' is the theme tune to which US television series?
10. The 1981 film 'Chariots of Fire' was based on the stories of which two British athletes?

Round 5

1. In which country was singer Frank Ifield born in November 1937?
2. What is mixed with soda water to make a spritzer?
3. By what name was Bold Jack Donohoe better known as a bushranger?
4. Shiitake is what type of foodstuff?
5. How many stars appear on the national flag of Kosovo?
6. A tridecagon has how many sides?
7. What is the highest number on an Australian X Lotto ticket?
8. A shoat, is the young of which animal?
9. How many contestants are at the start of the television quiz show 'The Chase'?
10. The radio adaptation of which H G Wells novel, narrated by Orson Welles caused panic in parts of the USA in October 1938?

Quiz Twenty-Bonus Round Questions

1. What is the middle name of cartoon character Daffy Duck?
2. Which school featured in UK TV's 'Please Sir'?
3. Which Scottish photographer took the famous 1969 photo of The Beatles on a zebra crossing on Abbey Road?

Answers Quiz Twenty

Round 1

1. Gnu
2. Steve McQueen
3. Iceland
4. Woodrow Wilson
5. Adam Ant
6. Queen Victoria
7. Jack of clubs
8. Anno Domini
9. Four
10. Lake Erie

Round 2

1. Five Euros
2. Skin
3. Benjamin Franklin
4. A A Milne
5. Georgie Porgie
6. Hydrogen peroxide
7. Sebastian
8. Lynryd Skynyrd
9. English
10. Eddie Fisher

Round 3

1. Q
2. Golda Meir
3. Icon
4. Blood poisoning
5. Eiger (North Face)
6. Roger
7. Al fresco
8. Richard Harris
9. Jabba the Hut
10. Australian Stock/ Securities Exchange

Round 4

1. John Major
2. Tuberculosis
3. 180
4. HG Wells
5. Zurich
6. Washington DC
7. Ireland
8. Ice hockey
9. Cheers
10. Harold Abrahams Eric Liddell

Round 5

1. England
2. Wine
3. Wild Colonial Boy
4. Mushroom
5. Six
6. 13
7. 49
8. Pig-newly weaned
9. Four
10. War of the Worlds

Quiz Twenty-Bonus Round Answers

1. Dumas
2. Fenn Street
3. Iain MacMillan

Quiz 21

Round 1

1. Which American state is nearest to the former Soviet Union?
2. In which city was Martin Luther King assassinated in 1968?
3. Who won six consecutive Wimbledon singles titles in the 1980s?
4. In which 1979 film was the spaceship called Nostromo?
5. Who wrote 'The Secret Diary of Adrian Mole'?
6. A 'Sloppy Joe' is an informal name for which item of clothing?
7. What was former British Prime Minister Margaret Thatcher's maiden name?
8. Equinophobia is the abnormal fear of which animals?
9. Which four letter word beginning with Y is the basic monetary unit of China, equal to 100 Fen?
10. The Montreux Jazz Festival is held annually in which European country?

Round 2

1. Pyongyang is the capital of which country?
2. In the Harry Potter series of books which animal is Hagrid allergic to?
3. Balmoral Castle is in which European country?
4. What was former Australian Prime Minister Gough Whitlam's first name?
5. The US television series 'The Wire' is set in which city?
6. What is the name of Rose Tyler's boyfriend in the UK television series 'Doctor Who'?
7. Who was the only Premier of an Australian state to have been dismissed from his post by the state governor?
8. The bull represents which sign of the Zodiac?
9. The Fountain of Wealth is in which Asian city?
10. Which three South American countries lie on the Equator?

Round 3

1. In the Star Wars series of films what is the name of the fictional weapon, consisting of a polished hilt which projects a blade of plasma, used by the Jedi and the Sith?
2. Gomito is Italian for which part of the body?
3. The Gardiner Dam is in which country?
4. In 1991, who took over from Ringo Starr to narrate the UK children's television series 'Thomas the Tank Engine and Friends'?
5. Romano is what type of foodstuff?
6. The Asteroid Belt lies between the orbits of which two planets in our solar system?
7. The first Summer Paralympic Games were hosted by which European city in 1960?

8. Ozzy Osbourne, lead singer and front man of the band Black Sabbath, was born in which British city?
9. In medicine, 'singultus' is more commonly known as what type of involuntary action in humans?
10. Which city has a university called the Sorbonne?

Round 4

1. What are said to be the last words of Julius Caesar?
2. Which fungus is an ingredient of bread?
3. Who had an album called Buddha and the Chocolate Box?
4. What two animals are associated with the stock market?
5. In Greek mythology, what is Pegasus?
6. What book details the rise of the simian empire at the expense of the human race?
7. In what country are the beaches of Normandy?
8. What was Australia's first TV station in 1956?
9. What is the southernmost state of the USA?
10. What should be around the rim of the glass when serving a margarita?

Round 5

1. Adolescence is considered to end at what age?
2. What colour shirts do referees wear in American football?
3. What is Australia's oldest musical instrument?
4. In what city is the Wailing Wall? J
5. What food causes the most allergic reactions in people?
6. What can't a vampire bear to smell?
7. In which Texas city is the Alamo?
8. Which Australian Prime Minister was nicknamed The Prefect?
9. How many letter tiles are there in a game of Scrabble?
10. Which Asian country has the longest school year?

Quiz Twenty One-Bonus Round Questions

1. In rugby union, how many tests did John Eales play for Australia?
2. Who became the first socialist Prime Minister of Greece in 1981?
3. In June 1991, which late US President was exhumed to test whether his death was caused by arsenic poisoning and not gastrointestinal illness?

Answers Quiz Twenty One

Round 1

1. Alaska
2. Memphis
3. Martina Navratilova
4. Alien
5. Sue Townsend
6. Jumper/sweater
7. Roberts
8. Horses
9. Yuan
10. Switzerland

Round 2

1. North Korea
2. Cats
3. Scotland
4. Edward
5. Baltimore
6. Mickey Smith
7. Jack Lang
8. Taurus
9. Singapore
10. Ecuador, Colombia Brazil

Round 3

1. Lightsaber
2. Elbow
3. Canada
4. Michael Angelis
5. Cheese
6. Mars & Jupiter
7. Rome
8. Birmingham
9. Hiccup
10. Paris

Round 4

1. Et tu, Brute
2. Yeast
3. Cat Stevens
4. Bulls and bears
5. A winged horse
6. Planet of the Apes
7. France
8. Channel 9
9. Hawaii
10. Salt

Round 5

1. 18
2. Black and white stripes
3. A didgeridoo
4. Jerusalem
5. Nuts
6. Garlic
7. San Antonio
8. Malcolm Fraser
9. 100
10. Japan

Quiz Twenty One-Bonus Round Answers

1. 86
2. Andreas Papandreou
3. Zachary Taylor

Quiz 22

Round 1

1. What is the name of Germany's official airline?
2. In what year did Princess Diana die?
3. On which mountain did Jesus take his last supper?
4. Which animal is on the golden Flemish flag?
5. For which narrow sea strait is Hellespont the ancient name?
6. Which Turkish city has the name of a cartoon character?
7. What is the noisiest city in the world?
8. What is the name of the desert area in Mexico?
9. Which river flows through Rome?
10. What island, which belonged to Denmark, became independent in 1944?

Round 2

1. On which continent can you visit Sierra Leone?
2. What is the second largest country in Europe after Russia?
3. What is the largest city in Canada?
4. In which city was the Titanic built?
5. Which city became capital of West-Germany in 1949?
6. When did Albania become an independent country? In 1813, 1853 or 1913?
7. Xerxes ruled a great empire around the fifth century BC. Which empire?
8. Which French king was called the Sun King?
9. What was in England the northern frontier of the Roman Empire?
10. Which two seas are joined by the Suez Canal?

Round 3

1. Which building in Athens was destroyed by a Venetian cannon ball in the 17th century?
2. What was the former name of New York?
3. Which city was the capital of Australia from 1901 to 1927?
4. Which country sent its navy around the world to fight the Japanese in 1904?
5. What is the most spoken language in Belgium?
6. In which country had the Orange Revolution between 2004-2005?
7. Which country had a Prime Minister and President who were twin brothers?
8. Which horse won the Melbourne Cup in 2002?
9. Who was the most recent Australian to win the men's singles title at Wimbledon?
10. How many gold medals did Australia win at the 2002 Winter Olympic Games?

Round 4

1. The symbol of which sign of the zodiac is that of a maiden, based on Astraea, the goddess of innocence and purity?
2. What is the name for the raised, enclosed platform located inside a church or a chapel from where the speaker will deliver a sermon?
3. Azeroth is a fictional planet found in which massively multiplayer online role-playing game- Ever Quest, Doom or World of Warcraft?
4. 'Here' is the sixth studio album from which American soul singer known for Songs in A Minor?
5. Which deal signed by 170 countries in early 2016, requires governments around the world to keep the global temperature rise to two degrees?
6. The Australian landmark Katu Tjuta is also known as what?
7. The Tamar River flows to which Tasmanian town/city?
8. How much of Australia is classified as desert A) 8% B) 16% C) 25% D) 35%
9. Andy Murray was World Tennis number one at 29 years old. He is the second oldest player to achieve this feat for this first time. Who was the oldest?
10. Which team in 2016 won Baseball's World Series for the first time since 1908?

Round 5

1. Which British coin changed its shape in 2017, becoming twelve-sided?
2. Which London public space commemorates a British naval victory in the Napoleonic Wars that took place on 21st October 1805?
3. What is the name of the project to search for evidence of life on Mars run by both the European Space Agency and a Russian space agency?
4. Which Ernest Hemingway novel features Robert Jordan, an American who has joined the International Brigades during the Spanish Civil War?
5. Which Caribbean island has the biggest population: Bahamas or Barbados?
6. Which German alcoholic drink translates into English as 'Hunting Master'?
7. Which American singer appeared as Johnny Tyronne in the 1965 musical comedy Harum Scarum?
8. What is Australia's largest non-salt lake?
9. Name Australia's western-most point?
10. Who won consecutive Gold Logies from 1997 to 2000?

Quiz Twenty Two-Bonus Round Questions

1. Who was the Portuguese dictator at the time of Franco?
2. What was the Latin name of Paris in Roman times?
3. Who was the first player to win 2 Brownlow Medals?

Answers Quiz Twenty Two

Round 1

1. Lufthansa
2. 1997
3. Golgotha or Calvary
4. Lion
5. Dardanelles
6. Batman
7. Hong Kong
8. Sonora
9. Tiber
10. Iceland

Round 2

1. Africa
2. France
3. Toronto
4. Belfast
5. Bonn
6. 1913
7. Persian Empire
8. Louis XIV
9. Hadrian's Wall
10. Mediterranean Sea
    Red Sea

Round 3

1. Parthenon
2. New Amsterdam
3. Melbourne
4. Russia
5. Dutch
6. Ukraine
7. Poland
8. Media Puzzle
9. Lleyton Hewitt
10. 2

Round 4

1. Virgo
2. Pulpit
3. World of Warcraft
4. Alicia Keys
5. Paris Agreement
6. The Olgas
7. Launceston
8. D-35%
9. John Newcombe (1974)
10. Chicago Cubs

Round 5

1. The £1 coin
2. Trafalgar Square
3. ExoMars
4. For Whom the Bell Tolls
5. Bahamas
6. Jagermeister
7. Elvis Presley
8. Lake Mackay, WA
9. Steep Point (Shark Bay)
10. Lisa McCune

Quiz Twenty Two-Bonus Round Answers

1. Salazar
2. Lutetia
3. Ivor Warne-Smith (1926/1928)

Quiz 23

Round 1

1. Which Apollo moon mission was the first to carry a lunar rover vehicle?
2. What is the only Central American country in which baseball, not soccer, is the people's favourite sport?
3. Tokelau is a dependency of which country?
4. In which 1951 film did Fred Astaire appear to dance on the ceiling?
5. In the TV show Family Guy, what is the name of the Griffins` lecherous neighbour?
6. In which European city can you find the home of Anne Frank?
7. How many stars has the American flag got?
8. What is the name of the Indian holy river?
9. What is the national animal of China?
10. What was the name of King Henry VIII`s older brother?

Round 2

1. How old was Prince Charles when he was invested as Prince of Wales?
2. What is the collective term for a group of racoons?
3. Which country had the name Rhodesia?
4. Which German war criminal was for 21 years the only inmate of Spandau prison?
5. What was the name of the Protestant revolution against the domination of the Pope?
6. What is the defoliant called that was used in Vietnam?
7. What is the only bird that is capable of seeing the colour blue?
8. Which was the first European country to issue banknotes?
9. What is the longest river in the Northern Territory?
10. What Australian movie includes the phrase "Tell him he's dreaming"?

Round 3

1. Who is older: Tony Blair or Theresa May?
2. Oscar Wilde said: "I can resist everything except..." what?
3. Who led the Red Army to victory over Germany in Berlin in 1945?
4. What song played during Scott and Charlene's wedding on Neighbours?
5. What is rupophobia the fear of?
6. Which is the second largest city in NSW?
7. Who is the longest serving presenter of Playschool?
8. Which sportsman`s autobiography is called `My Side`?
9. How many eyes does a bee have?
10. In the 2016 film Nice Guys, which two Hollywood actors are the film's 'nice guys'?

Round 4

1. What name is given to the cabin below an Airship?
2. How old was the character of Dorothy in the film `The Wizard of Oz`?
3. Who is the second most mentioned man in the Bible?
4. What is South Australia's largest island?
5. What is the tallest waterfall in Australia?
6. Who did Ireland's rugby union team defeat for the first time in November 2016?
7. Which singer received a Lifetime Achievement Award at the 50th Country Music Awards in Nashville?
8. What is the most common surname in Spain?
9. Which `P. M. ` is the name of the lawyer who never loses a case in `The Flintstones`?
10. What is the only mobile national monument in the USA?

Round 5

1. What was actor Joaquin Phoenix's original Christian name?
2. Dinosaurs became extinct at the end of which period?
3. How old was Elvis Presley when he had his first number one single?
4. What was the name of the dog that befriended Kevin Costner in `Dances with Wolves`?
5. Which 'T' word describes the way that an object feels to the touch?
6. Which British pop group had a 1982 number one single with 'My Camera Never Lies'?
7. In which 1847 novel would you find the character Heathcliff?
8. In which decade was John F. Kennedy born?
9. Which 'b' word is a salted water used to preserve food?
10. Which Australian director was nominated for an Oscar for the 1998 film `The Truman Show`?

Quiz Twenty Three-Bonus Round Questions

1. How long, in kilometres, is the Suez Canal?
2. In which year did Pablo Picasso die?
3. What does digamy mean?

Answers Quiz Twenty Three

Round 1

1. Apollo 15
2. Nicaragua
3. New Zealand
4. Royal Wedding
5. Glenn Quagmire
6. Amsterdam
7. Fifty
8. Ganges
9. Giant panda
10. Arthur

Round 2

1. 20
2. A nursery
3. Zimbabwe
4. Rudolf Hess
5. Reformation
6. Agent Orange
7. The owl
8. Sweden
9. Victoria River
10. The Castle

Round 3

1. Tony Blair
2. Temptation
3. Georgi Zhukov
4. Suddenly
5. Rubbish or dirt
6. Newcastle
7. Benita Collings
8. David Beckham's
9. 5
10. Russell Crowe & Ryan Reynolds

Round 4

1. Gondola
2. 17
3. David
4. Kangaroo Island
5. Wallaman Falls, QLD
6. New Zealand
7. Dolly Parton
8. Garcia
9. Perry Masonry
10. Cable cars in San Francisco

Round 5

1. Leaf
2. The Cretaceous
3. 21
4. Two Socks
5. Texture
6. Bucks Fizz
7. Wuthering Heights
8. 1910s (1917)
9. Brine
10. Peter Weir

Quiz Twenty Three-Bonus Round Answers

1. 163
2. 1973
3. A second legal marriage after the death or divorce of the first husband or wife

Quiz 24

Round 1

1. A macchiato is a type of what?
2. Which two forms of warfare were outlawed under the Geneva Convention of 1925?
3. Who was the German chancellor at the time of the Unification of Germany in 1990?
4. Who is the only driver to have held both the Formula 1 World Championship and the Indy World Series at the same time?
5. What colour is the skin of a polar bear?
6. In which Disney animation does the song "Zero to Hero" feature?
7. Who was the last Labour Prime Minister of Great Britain? (as of 2019)
8. For what is the Spanish town of Toledo famous for manufacturing?
9. In the 2009 animated TV film of "The Gruffalo" who provided the voice of the Gruffalo?
10. Which song gave Queen their first US number one?

Round 2

1. Of what creatures is Alektorophobia the irrational fear?
2. What is the name of the murderer in the 1978 movie "Halloween"?
3. What was the last Bond film made starring Pierce Brosnan?
4. Which canal was completed in 1869?
5. How many lifeboats were on the Titanic's maiden voyage?
6. The emerald is the birthstone for what month?
7. After how many years of marriage would you celebrate a leather wedding anniversary?
8. What is the name of The Jetsons` dog?
9. What animal has the heaviest and most complex brain in the animal world?
10. Who was the first Roman Catholic to become American President?

Round 3

1. What city was the first in the southern hemisphere to host the Olympics?
2. Which famous actress once said `I`ve been in more laps than a napkin`?
3. Which planet in the Solar System is closest in size to Earth?
4. Which Australian city was founded in 1829?
5. What type of food is basmati?

6. Anthony Stark is the alter-ego of which super-hero?
7. On which side of the road do people drive in Japan?
8. Fort Knox lies in which American state?
9. Who was assassinated by Nathuram Godse in 1948?
10. Who has written a series of letters entitled `Dear Fatty` in the form of an autobiography?

Round 4

1. What is made using soda, lime and silica?
2. What is the speed limit on a German motorway?
3. Which world famous musician was born Farrokh Bulsara in Zanzibar in 1946?
4. What building is pictured on a bottle of HP sauce?
5. A country historically known as Abyssinia, what is the modern name for it?
6. In Peter Pan, what is the name of Captain Hook`s ship?
7. Which singer had hits with Rubber Ball and The Night Has a Thousand Eyes?
8. What sized ball is a game of netball played with?
9. Who assassinated John Lennon?
10. What country was formerly known as Persia?

Round 5

1. What is the capital city of Tasmania?
2. What shape is the road sign `Stop`?
3. In what year was the Great Train Robbery?
4. What was the nickname given to the famous boxing match between Mohammad Ali and Joe Frazier in1975?
5. What is the capital of the Caribbean island of Grenada?
6. Which football team are known as the Rosso-Neri?
7. The 1999 film 10 Things I Hate About You is based on which Shakespeare play?
8. Where in the body would you find an astrocyte?
9. The 1812 Overture was written to celebrate the defeat of Napoleon in which city?
10. Who wrote the Sinead O`Connor hit Nothing Compares 2 U?

Quiz Twenty Four-Bonus Round Questions

1. How many surfaces does a Mobius strip have?
2. Before Clive Palmer, who was the last leader of the United Australia Party?
3. Including interim leaders, how Federal leaders did the Australian Democrats have?

Answers Quiz Twenty Four

Round 1

1. Espresso coffee
2. Biological & Chemical
3. Helmut Kohl
4. Nigel Mansell
5. Black
6. Hercules
7. Gordon Brown
8. Swords
9. Robbie Coltrane
10. Crazy Little Thing Called Love

Round 2

1. Chickens
2. Michael Myers
3. Die Another Day
4. The Suez Canal
5. 20
6. May
7. 3
8. Astro
9. The sperm whale
10. John F Kennedy

Round 3

1. Melbourne
2. Mae West
3. Venus
4. Perth
5. Rice
6. Iron-Man
7. The left side
8. Kentucky
9. Mahatma Gandhi
10. Dawn French

Round 4

1. Glass
2. No Limit
3. Freddie Mercury
4. Houses of Parliament
5. Ethiopia
6. Jolly Roger
7. Bobby Vee
8. Size 5
9. Mark Chapman
10. Iran

Round 5

1. Hobart
2. Octagonal
3. 1963
4. Thrilla in Manila
5. St George's
6. AC Milan
7. Taming of the Shrew
8. The brain
9. Moscow
10. Prince

Quiz Twenty Four-Bonus Round answers

1. One
2. Robert Menzies
3. 11

Quiz 25

Round 1

1. What is the world`s northernmost capital city?
2. In the Bourne films starring Matt Damon what is Bourne`s first name?
3. Which South American country hosted the 2014 FIFA World Cup?
4. In which North American city is there a neighbourhood known as Hell`s Kitchen?
5. In which city were the 1940 Olympic Games scheduled to take place before being cancelled due to war?
6. In which Australian state would you find the Barossa Valley?
7. Which pop singer did Debbie Rowe marry?
8. To which country does the territory of Christmas Island belong?
9. In musical notes, which is bigger - a crotchet or a semibreve?
10. What is the capital of Iran?

Round 2

1. What nationality was Mozart?
2. In which Australian State or Territory would you find the Adelaide River?
3. The name of which Italian cheese means `recooked`?
4. Which singer had a string of hits in the 1970s and is often referred to as the `Queen of Disco`?
5. Where did the peaceful Velvet Revolution take place in 1989?
6. When the UN was established in 1945, what did it replace?
7. Which group had a number one album in 1979 with Regatta De Blanc?
8. The Nursery End, the Pavilion End and St John`s Road are all linked with which sporting ground?
9. Which is the only US state not to have a straight line in its borders?
10. Who is the hero in the best-selling novel The Da Vinci Code?

Round 3

1. Which is the second largest US state by area?
2. Who plays Count Olaf in the film Lemony Snicket`s A Series Of Unfortunate Events'?
3. Which American state is home to the Timberwolves, the Twins and the Vikings?
4. Who is Kate Hudson`s famous actress mother?
5. In which war were the most Victoria Crosses awarded?

6. Which TV series featured the character Eliot Ness?
7. In which religion is Vishnu worshipped as the God of creation?
8. What is the capital of Uruguay?
9. In Doctor Who, who was the creator of the Daleks?
10. What is the name of the character of the cultural attaché portrayed by Barry Humphries?

Round 4

1. Who comes next in the following sequence? John, Paul, John Paul, John Paul II?
2. What name is given to a cow that has not had a calf?
3. What name did Tom Hanks give to his volleyball companion in the film `Cast Away`?
4. Who is the most nominated male actor for an Oscar?
5. Who was Maxwell Smart's main KAOS nemesis?
6. What was the name of the opponent that Mike Tyson bit the ear lobe off?
7. What is the name given to the green alkaline fluid produced by the liver?
8. Which Queen had been pregnant at least 17 times, but only gave birth to one child who lived to be at least 2 years old?
9. In the TV show `The Saint` what was the full name of the main character?
10. The Battle of Bunker Hill was fought during which war?

Round 5

1. What was the name of the housekeeper in Father Ted?
2. What name is given to a native of Sydney, Australia?
3. Which bird lays the biggest egg in the world?
4. In motoring, what does MG stand for?
5. What pirate sailed the ship The Queen Anne`s Revenge?
6. What colour is the bottom stripe on the Croatian flag?
7. What was the name of the character that O J Simpson played in the `Naked Gun` films?
8. How many players are there in a Handball team?
9. What is the only venomous mammal in the world?
10. What is Europe`s highest capital city?

Quiz Twenty Five-Bonus Round Questions

1. How many people signed the American Declaration of Independence?
2. In what year B.C. was Alexander the Great born?
3. Which American state first declared Labor Day a legal holiday?

Answers Quiz Twenty Five

Round 1

1. Reykjavik
2. Jason
3. Brazil
4. New York
5. Tokyo
6. South Australia
7. Michael Jackson
8. Australia
9. Semibreve
10. Tehran

Round 2

1. Austrian
2. Northern Territory
3. Ricotta
4. Donna Summer
5. Czechoslovakia
6. League of Nations
7. The Police
8. Lords
9. Hawaii
10. Professor Robert Langdon

Round 3

1. Texas
2. Jim Carrey
3. Minnesota
4. Goldie Hawn
5. First World War
6. The Untouchables
7. Hinduism
8. Montevideo
9. Davros
10. Sir Les Patterson

Round 4

1. Benedict
2. A heifer
3. Wilson
4. Jack Nicholson
5. Siegfried
6. Evander Holyfield
7. Bile
8. Queen Anne
9. Simon Templar
10. American War of Independence

Round 5

1. Mrs Doyle
2. Sydneysider
3. The ostrich
4. Morris Garages
5. Edward Teach (aka Blackbeard)
6. Blue
7. Officer Nordberg
8. 7
9. The duckbill platypus
10. Madrid

Quiz Twenty Five-Bonus Round Answers

1. 56
2. 356 BC
3. Colorado

Quiz 26

Round 1

1. In what year was David Beckham born?
2. Are mammals cold blooded or warm blooded?
3. What are the Sons of Anarchy?
4. What is usually sold at reduced prices during a happy hour?
5. In which city is Tiananmen Square?
6. In which city did rhyming slang originate?
7. Who was the last Beatle to marry twice?
8. What kind of animal is Eeyore in the Winnie the Pooh books?
9. What flower is associated with Remembrance Day?
10. What note follows the musical note 'soh'?

Round 2

1. Who wrote 'The Ugly Duckling'?
2. Who wears a chasuble?
3. Which song starts, 'Friday night and the lights are low'?
4. Emphysema affects which part of the body?
5. What were cricketer WG Grace's first two names?
6. Why does a glow worm glow?
7. In the song, what colour rose is linked to Texas?
8. How many holes are most major golf tournaments played over?
9. Which spirit is Pimm's No. 1 based on?
10. What is examined using an otoscope?

Round 3

1. In which US state is Death Valley?
2. What do alligators lay their eggs in?
3. December begins in which star sign?
4. Machu Picchu is in which mountain range?
5. Which sea is the least salty in the world?
6. What colour are Scrabble tiles?
7. What name is given to a young seal?
8. Which pop star calls her fans 'little monsters?
9. What is the study of handwriting called?
10. In which Australian city is the Festival Theatre?

Round 4

1. Who was the main actor in the film 'The King's Speech'?
2. Who was the British Prime Minister before David Cameron?
3. Which animated film introduced the Minions?
4. An elver is a young what?
5. Which Gilbert and Sullivan opera is set in Venice?
6. Who was manager of Chelsea before Jose Mourinho came in 2004?
7. In which month is Thanksgiving celebrated in America?
8. What is the opposite of an acid?
9. Where do mosquitoes lay their eggs?
10. Toronto is the capital of which Canadian province?

Round 5

1. What is the skin on a deer's antlers called?
2. Which English king bought Buckingham Palace?
3. What number President of the USA is Donald Trump?
4. Lard is produced mainly from what animal?
5. What is scree on a mountainside?
6. What is a sumo wrestling ring made from?
7. What colour are Mickey Mouse's gloves?
8. What is added to Galliano to make a Harvey Wallbanger?
9. What is the metric word for million?
10. Which element has the highest boiling point?

Quiz Twenty Six-Bonus Round Questions

1. Who was Mary O'Brien better known as in pop music?
2. What is a young penguin called
3. What percentage of all living mammals are rodents?

Answers Quiz Twenty Six

Round 1

1. 1975
2. Warm blooded
3. A motorcycle gang
4. Drinks
5. Beijing
6. London
7. Paul McCartney
8. Donkey
9. Poppy
10. Lah

Round 2

1. Hans Christian Anderson
2. A priest
3. Dancing Queen
4. Lungs
5. William Gilbert
6. To attract mates
7. Yellow
8. 72
9. Gin
10. Ear

Round 3

1. California
2. Sand
3. Sagittarius
4. The Andes
5. Baltic Sea
6. Cream
7. Pup
8. Lady Gaga
9. Calligraphy
10. Adelaide

Round 4

1. Colin Firth
2. Gordon Brown
3. 'Despicable Me'
4. Eel
5. The Gondoliers
6. Claudio Ranieri
7. November
8. An alkali
9. In water
10. Ontario

Round 5

1. Velvet
2. George III
3. 45th
4. Pigs
5. Loose rocks
6. Clay
7. White
8. Vodka and orange juice
9. Mega
10. Carbon

Quiz Twenty Six-Bonus Round Answers

1. Dusty Springfield
2. A chick
3. 40%

Quiz 27

Round 1

1. What colour is carmine?
2. Who had the 2014 hit single 'Happy'?
3. How many colours are in the spectrum?
4. How many seasons did Louis Suarez play for Liverpool?
5. Which city is served by Kingsford Smith airport?
6. Which four letters preface access to an internet address?
7. Which pink bird sleeps on one leg?
8. Who played the character Dame Edna Everage?
9. What is the wife of a sultan called?
10. What word describes something being next to last?

Round 2

1. Who was the lead singer of T Rex?
2. Which team won the first FA Cup decided on penalties?
3. What is the highest female singing voice?
4. What was Ted in the film 'Ted'?
5. Who was the first Republican President of the United States?
6. How many wings does a moth have?
7. What country is golfer Ernie Els from?
8. In which US state is the Paul Getty Museum?
9. Who wrote the book Das Kapital?
10. What note does an orchestra tune to?

Round 3

1. Who became Australian Prime Minister in 1975?
2. What colour is cayenne pepper?
3. What city does singer Kylie Minogue come from?
4. Who was the Canadian Prime Minister before Justin Trudeau?
5. Which country was the first to legalise abortion?
6. What export industry is the NSW city of Newcastle most associated with today?
7. Who wrote the opera Carmen?
8. What colour is a male blue mandrill's behind?
9. What are the sticks used in a game of hurling called?
10. What colour was the original Model T Ford?

Round 4

1. What was the name of the bad tempered magical tree in the Harry Potter stories?
2. What is squared in Albert Einstein's famous formula for relativity?
3. Melanin is the primary determinant of a person's what?
4. What type of animal is a schnauzer?
5. Bjorn was married to which member of ABBA?
6. Which famous French mime artist died in 2007?
7. Who had a 1990s hit with the song 'Black or White'?
8. What does SUV stand for?
9. Emeralds are a variety of which mineral?
10. How many pylons does the Sydney Harbour Bridge have?

Round 5

1. What is a type of fruit as well as a part of your body?
2. What is the common name for sodium bicarbonate?
3. What does the abbreviation ROM stand for?
4. What did the lion lack in the Wizard of Oz?
5. What is the groove pattern on a tyre called?
6. What facial feature does the Mona Lisa lack?
7. How many lines in a sonnet?
8. What is another name for a lexicon?
9. Who starred as Jessica Simpson's husband in the reality show 'Newlyweds'?
10. What two words is Pokémon a contraction of?

Twenty Seven-Bonus Round Questions

1. Who said, 'There never was a good war, nor a bad peace?
2. What relation to King Arthur was Mordred?
3. In which sport is there a bonspiel?

Answers Quiz Twenty Seven

Round 1

1. Red
2. Pharrell Williams
3. Seven
4. Four
5. Sydney
6. http
7. Flamingo
8. Barry Humphries
9. Sultana
10. Penultimate

Round 2

1. Marc Bolan
2. Arsenal
3. Soprano
4. A teddy bear
5. Abraham Lincoln
6. Four
7. South Africa
8. California
9. Karl Marx
10. A

Round 3

1. Malcolm Fraser
2. Red
3. Melbourne
4. Stephen Harper
5. Iceland
6. Coal
7. Bizet
8. Blue
9. Hurleys
10. Black

Round 4

1. Whomping Willow
2. C
3. Skin
4. Dog
5. Agnetha
6. Marcel Marceau
7. Michael Jackson
8. Sports Utility Vehicle
9. Beryl
10. Four

Round 5

1. Navel
2. Baking soda
3. Read Only Memory
4. Courage
5. Tread
6. Eyebrows
7. 14
8. A dictionary
9. Nick Lachey
10. Pocket monster

Quiz Twenty Seven-Bonus Round Answers

1. Benjamin Franklin
2. Nephew
3. Curling

Quiz 28

Round 1

1. What group was Beyoncé a part of?
2. Who wrote the book 'Black Beauty'?
3. What can a chameleon lizard change?
4. What are the colours of the Austrian flag?
5. Which country lies immediately east of Chile?
6. What is the name given to the building where whiskey is made?
7. Which English king was called 'The Confessor'?
8. What are the bars on a xylophone made from?
9. In which US state is Palm Springs?
10. Which city is the most northerly capital in Europe?

Round 2

1. What colour is the skin of a kiwi fruit?
2. How many bones does a slug have?
3. What is the German word for the number seven?
4. What is the New Zealand rugby union team called?
5. What would you do with a sitar?
6. With which sport do we associate a half nelson?
7. Where did the dance the rumba originate?
8. How many points does a snowflake have?
9. What is the capital of the Australian state of Queensland?
10. In which decade was the first American Superbowl?

Round 3

1. Which country had a private security force called the Tonton Macoutes?
2. Which railway links Russia with the Pacific Ocean?
3. What is the only anagram of the word English?
4. What is the world's largest gulf?
5. What is the flavour of ouzo?
6. What percentage is half of a half?
7. Who was the original singer of the group INXS?
8. How many sides does a trapezium have?
9. Which western movie star had a horse called Champion?
10. Which musician had the nickname 'Satchmo'?

Round 4

1. What have you betrayed if you commit treason?
2. What does a chronometer measure?
3. In which sea is Jamaica?
4. What is the calm centre of a hurricane called?
5. A strudel is usually filled with which fruit?
6. What does the F stand for in FAQ?
7. At which park is Princess Diana buried?
8. In which US city is the Capitol Building?
9. Which country had 11 kings named Ramses?
10. How many seconds in half an hour?

Round 5

1. In which film did Michael Douglas say 'Greed is good'?
2. What is a gallivat?
3. What was the name of the U2 album given away with iTunes in 2014?
4. What is the German name for Bavaria?
5. Who was older when he died, John Lennon or Elvis Presley?
6. How high is a netball post?
7. Jazz musician John Coltrane played which instrument?
8. What type of creature is a flying fox?
9. What is another name for hypertension?
10. What is the official language of the Ivory Coast?

Quiz Twenty Eight-Bonus Round Questions

1. What was the name of King William IVs Queen?
2. A zinfandel is used for making what?
3. Which island is in the middle of Niagara Falls?

Answers Quiz Twenty Eight

Round 1

1. Destiny's Child
2. Anna Sewell
3. Colour
4. Red and white
5. Argentina
6. Distillery
7. Edward
8. Wood
9. California
10. Reykjavik

Round 2

1. Brown
2. None
3. Sieben
4. All blacks
5. Play it
6. Wrestling
7. Cuba
8. 6
9. Brisbane
10. 1960s

Round 3

1. Haiti
2. Trans-Siberian
3. Shingle
4. Gulf of Mexico
5. Aniseed
6. 25%
7. Michael Hutchence
8. Four
9. Gene Autry
10. Louis Armstrong

Round 4

1. Your country
2. Time
3. Caribbean
4. The eye
5. Apple
6. Frequently
7. Althorp Park
8. Washington DC
9. Egypt
10. 1800

Round 5

1. Wall Street
2. A boat
3. Songs of Innocence
4. Bayern
5. Elvis Presley
6. 10 feet (3.05m)
7. Saxophone
8. A bat
9. High blood pressure
10. French

Quiz Twenty Eight-Bonus Round Answers

1. Adelaide
2. Wine
3. Goat Island

Quiz 29

Round 1

1. Which famous screen dancer is on the cover of Sgt Pepper's album?
2. What type of country is Monaco?
3. How many strings are on a violin?
4. What instrument did Larry Adler play?
5. How many leaves are on a shamrock?
6. What does XLIV stand for in Roman Numerals?
7. Who was the Australian Prime Minister before Malcolm Turnbull?
8. On which river is the Niagara Falls?
9. FC Porto plays football in which country?
10. Which Disney film includes the song 'Let it Go'?

Round 2

1. What kind of animal is a fox terrier?
2. Chapatti is an Indian type of what?
3. Which Dire Straits song begins with 'Here comes Johnny'?
4. What do you watch on Gogglebox?
5. What is mined at Kimberley in South Africa?
6. Is a tulip grown from a bulb or seeds?
7. What is curling played on?
8. Which group was featured in the movie 'The Great Rock 'n' Roll Swindle'?
9. What was Bing Crosby's first name?
10. On which racecourse is the Melbourne Cup run?

Round 3

1. If you nictitate at someone, what are you doing?
2. Which disease was called phthisis?
3. Which religious group founded the city of Philadelphia?
4. What is New Zealand's national day called?
5. Who became the face of Estee Lauder in the mid-1990s?
6. Cos and iceberg are varieties of which salad plant?
7. What colour is Shrek?
8. How many hooks are used in crochet?
9. Which organ is affected by hepatitis?
10. What kind of animal is a chamois?

Round 4

1. In which city is Pushkin Square?
2. In which part of the UK is 'Trainspotting' set?
3. What nationality is the actor Sir Anthony Hopkins?
4. At which ceremony is a monarch given the throne?
5. Who played Jessica Fletcher in 'Murder She Wrote'?
6. In which UK city were Oasis formed?
7. What sport did Gabriela Sabatini play?
8. Who portrays the character Jonathan Creek?
9. Who did Nelson Mandela share the 1993 Nobel Peace Prize with?
10. In which country was Joan of Arc born?

Round 5

1. Which famous monument was built by Shah Jahan?
2. What is the common name for the clavicle?
3. What does Bass Strait divide?
4. Where was Checkpoint Charlie?
5. How many times did Joe Frazier fight Muhammad Ali?
6. If a creature is demersal, where does it live?
7. Who was called the Iron Chancellor?
8. Which property scandal of the 1990s implicated the Clintons?
9. On which sea is the Gaza Strip?
10. In what year was Trump Tower opened in New York?

Quiz Twenty Nine-Bonus Round Questions

1. Which English soccer club were the first to have 105 points in a season?
2. Who won the first cycling World Cup?
3. What was the name of the horse that was made a Roman consul?

Answers Quiz Twenty Nine

Round 1

1. Fred Astaire
2. Principality
3. Four
4. Harmonica
5. Three
6. Forty four
7. Tony Abbott
8. Niagara River
9. Portugal
10. Frozen

Round 2

1. Dog
2. Bread
3. Walk of Life
4. People watching TV
5. Diamonds
6. A bulb
7. Ice
8. The Sex Pistols
9. Harry
10. Flemington

Round 3

1. Winking
2. Tuberculosis
3. Quakers
4. Waitangi Day
5. Elizabeth Hurley
6. Lettuce
7. Green
8. One
9. Liver
10. Goat-antelope

Round 4

1. Moscow
2. Scotland
3. Welsh
4. Coronation
5. Angela Lansbury
6. Manchester
7. Tennis
8. Alan Davies
9. FW de Klerk
10. France

Round 5

1. Taj Mahal
2. Collar bone
3. Australia and Tasmania
4. Between East and West Berlin
5. Three
6. On the seabed
7. Otto Bismarck
8. Whitewater
9. Mediterranean
10. 1983

Quiz Twenty Nine-Bonus Round Answers

1. Reading
2. Sean Kelly
3. Incitatus

Quiz 30

Round 1

1. What is the abbreviation for the word volt?
2. Where is the door on a chest freezer?
3. What does the ply on a yarn refer to?
4. Which team did Tim Cahill play for in the Premier League?
5. Who had a daughter named Lourdes Maria in 1996?
6. In which country is Botany Bay?
7. How many players can a team have on the field in a game of gridiron?
8. Who was the Roman God of the sea?
9. In which country was the series 'Father Ted' set?
10. Who played Muhammad Ali in the film 'Ali'?

Round 2

1. How many minutes are there in a round of professional boxing?
2. Which animals do sailors say desert a sinking ship?
3. Which chess piece is shaped like a horse's head?
4. Whose official plane is Air Force One?
5. In which ocean is Fiji?
6. How many Gospels are there in the New Testament?
7. What is the layer around the Earth called?
8. Where is a bird's patella?
9. Who was the lead guitarist of Led Zeppelin?
10. Who wrote the play 'Private Lives'?

Round 3

1. What are you doing if you are mendicanting?
2. What is a firebrat?
3. What was James Dean's middle name?
4. Ellis Island is in which harbour?
5. In which century was the Battle of Agincourt?
6. Who wrote the Noddy books?
7. What colour is the Great Spot on Jupiter?
8. What travels at 186,272 miles per second?
9. What is the oldest university in England?
10. In which Italian city is the Rialto Bridge?

Round 4

1. Which bird was taken to work by miners to test for gas?
2. What are the official two languages of the Channel Islands?
3. Which letter represents 007's boss?
4. In what sport is a shuttlecock used?
5. What is measured by a pedometer?
6. In which country was Ayrton Senna born?
7. If January 1st was a Thursday, what day would February 1st be?
8. What country does golfer Mark Leishman come from?
9. How many Australian states have South in their name?
10. Who won the last World Cup of soccer in the 20th century?

Round 5

1. Where did karaoke singing originate?
2. What is the collective name for a litter of piglets?
3. Who was Mata Hari executed by?
4. What is the capital of the Canadian province of Manitoba?
5. Who had No. 1 singles in the 1980s with Queen and Mick Jagger?
6. In metres, how long is the Melbourne Cup horse race?
7. Which cartoon character had a friend called Boo Boo?
8. Who played Truman in The Truman Show?
9. In which country was Idi Amin Prime Minister?
10. Who is buried at the Arc de Triomphe in Paris?

Quiz Thirty-Bonus Round Questions

1. How many 'Road' Movies were made?
2. The town of Carrara in Italy is famous for what?
3. Who was Prince Phillip's father?

Answers Quiz Thirty

Round 1

1. V
2. On top
3. Its thickness
4. Everton
5. Madonna
6. Australia
7. Eleven
8. Neptune
9. Ireland
10. Will Smith

Round 2

1. Three
2. Rats
3. The knight
4. President of USA
5. Pacific
6. Four
7. Atmosphere
8. The knee
9. Jimmy Paige
10. Noel Coward

Round 3

1. Begging
2. Insect
3. Byron
4. New York
5. 15th
6. Enid Blyton
7. Red
8. Light
9. Oxford
10. Venice

Round 4

1. Canaries
2. English & French
3. M
4. Badminton
5. Walking distance
6. Brazil
7. Sunday
8. Australia
9. Two
10. France

Round 5

1. Japan
2. Farrow
3. The French
4. Winnipeg
5. David Bowie
6. 3200m
7. Yogi Bear
8. Jim Carrey
9. Uganda
10. The Unknown Soldier

Quiz Thirty-Bonus Round Answers

1. Seven
2. White marble
3. Prince Andrew of Greece

Quiz 31

Round 1

1. Who wrote 'Charlie and the Chocolate Factory'?
2. Do bananas grow pointing up or down?
3. Is an Afghan hound long or short haired?
4. What were the initials for US President Lyndon Johnson?
5. In which country were BMWs first made?
6. What is pram the abbreviation of?
7. Who founded the PLO?
8. In what year did Brad Pitt and Angelina Jolie marry?
9. Which country's rugby union team is called the Wallabies?
10. What country was once called Cathay?

Round 2

1. In what year did Marilyn Monroe die?
2. What colour is azure?
3. What are DC 10s and 747s?
4. In which European country is the town of Spa?
5. In football, what is the main colour of Holland's shirts?
6. How many Teletubbies are there?
7. Who played the part of Rachel in 'Friends'?
8. Who produced most of the Beatles' songs?
9. What sort of creature is a fluke?
10. How is the wife of a knight addressed?

Round 3

1. In which two countries is the Dead Sea?
2. Who painted Starry Night?
3. What shape is a sumo wrestling ring?
4. What describes descending a sheer face by sliding down a rope?
5. What is the fear of enclosed spaces called?
6. What sport do the Chicago Bears play?
7. What is Australia's largest lake?
8. Who came from the planet Ork?
9. At which Olympics was Ben Johnson disqualified for drug taking?
10. What was the title of Ike and Tina Turner's only album?

Round 4

1. In which city was John Lennon murdered?
2. How many English Kings have been named Stephen?
3. Who lived in the mansion Graceland?
4. Before he was married, was Prince Phillip in the army or navy?
5. What country was the centre of operations for the Taliban?
6. What does the B stand for in LBW in cricket?
7. Which of the Spice Girls wore a Union Jack dress?
8. Who won the Brownlow Medal in Australian football in 2016?
9. What side of a ship is starboard?
10. Who had a hit with 'Uptown Funk'?

Round 5

1. Who hit six sixes in an over of cricket in 1968?
2. Which Star Trek star died in February 2015?
3. What is the name of Mr Addams in 'The Addams Family'?
4. Which US hurdler was undefeated in 122 races?
5. What colour is the tongue of a giraffe?
6. Who provided the voice of the baby boy in Look Who's Talking?
7. Where is the Sea of Vapours?
8. What does BHP stand for?
9. Who was Mr Universe from 1968 to 1970?
10. The word ketchup comes from which language?

Quiz Thirty One-Bonus Round Questions

1. Which mammal lives at the highest altitude?
2. When can a woman suffer puerperal fever?
3. In what year did Benito Mussolini become Prime Minister in Italy?

Answers Quiz Thirty One

Round 1

1. Roald Dahl
2. Up
3. Long haired
4. LBJ
5. Germany
6. Perambulator
7. Yasser Arafat
8. 2014
9. Australia
10. China

Round 2

1. 1962
2. Blue
3. Aircraft
4. Belgium
5. Orange
6. Four
7. Jennifer Aniston
8. George Martin
9. Worm
10. Lady

Round 3

1. Israel & Jordan
2. Vincent van Gogh
3. Circular
4. Abseiling
5. Claustrophobia
6. Gridiron
7. Lake Eyre
8. Mork
9. Seoul 1988
10. River Deep Mountain High

Round 4

1. New York
2. One
3. Elvis Presley
4. Navy
5. Afghanistan
6. Before
7. Geri Halliwell/Ginger
8. Patrick Dangerfield
9. Right
10. Mark Ronson feat. Bruno Mars

Round 5

1. Garfield Sobers
2. Leonard Nimoy
3. Gomez
4. Edwin Moses
5. Blue
6. Bruce Willis
7. The moon
8. Broken Hill Proprietary
9. Arnold Schwarzenegger
10. Chinese

Quiz Thirty One-Bonus Round Answers

1. Mount Everest pika
2. After childbirth
3. 1922

Quiz 32

Round 1

1. Who won the Formula One Championship in 2016?
2. Whose headquarters are at Scotland Yard?
3. In which country is Boca Juniors football club?
4. Who is the Vice President of the USA? (as of 2020)
5. To which city will the Oakland Raiders gridiron team relocate?
6. What is the capital city of Trinidad and Tobago?
7. In what year was Madonna born?
8. In what year did Michael Jackson die?
9. The TV series 'ER' was set in which city?
10. What are the three colours on the German flag?

Round 2

1. What type of creature is a shrike?
2. What country does Monaco border?
3. What colour are a daisy's petals?
4. Which type of cat has a mane?
5. What type of animal is the star of 'Pingu'?
6. Which word means ghosts and a type of strong drink?
7. In which sport was Alex Jesaulenko a famous player?
8. What language was spoken by the ancient Romans?
9. Who played Stephen Hawking in 'The Theory of Everything'?
10. Which singer's real name is Curtis Jackson?

Round 3

1. The Ashanti tribe live in which African country?
2. In which city was tennis player Monica Seles stabbed?
3. Who played the title character in Remington Steele?
4. What is the capital of the Canadian province Alberta?
5. Game of Thrones is set in which fictional continent?
6. Where is the film 'The Mummy Returns' set?
7. What is Barbie's usual hair colour?
8. What can be a musical sound or a short letter?
9. What is caviar?
10. Which family had a hit with 'Do the Bartman'?

Round 4

1. What is the main ingredient of sauerkraut?
2. How many of Henry VIII's six wives were beheaded?
3. Who was the voice of Gru in 'Despicable Me'?
4. Hr. is the abbreviation of what?
5. Which was the second country to send a man into space?
6. What type of creature is a mandrill?
7. Who was Australian PM at the time of the new millennium?
8. What type of pattern is on a raccoon's tail?
9. Which constellation is known as The Hunter?
10. Dijon is what type of condiment?

Round 5

1. Who telephoned Neil Armstrong during his moon walk?
2. Who is the patron saint of Venice?
3. What type of a plant is a fescue?
4. What is the largest island in Asia?
5. What type of sugar is found in milk?
6. Who had a hit with 'Cotton Eye Joe'?
7. What is kelp?
8. In the play, who killed Macbeth?
9. Mesopotamia was the ancient name for which modern day country?
10. Alphabetically, which is the last chemical element?

Quiz Thirty Two-Bonus Round Questions

1. Which Henry became King of England in 1100?
2. What is a paravane used for?
3. Who led the Expedition of the Thousand in 1860?

Answers Quiz Thirty Two

Round 1

1. Nico Rosberg
2. English metropolitan police
3. Argentina
4. Mike Pence
5. Las Vegas
6. Port of Spain
7. 1958
8. 2009
9. Chicago
10. Black, red, yellow

Round 2

1. Bird
2. France
3. White
4. Lion
5. Penguin
6. Spirits
7. Australian football
8. Latin
9. Eddie Redmayne
10. 50 cent

Round 3

1. Ghana
2. Hamburg
3. Pierce Brosnan
4. Edmonton
5. Westeros
6. Egypt
7. Blonde
8. Note
9. Roe (fish eggs)
10. The Simpsons

Round 4

1. Cabbage
2. Two
3. Steve Carell
4. Hour
5. USA
6. Monkey
7. John Howard
8. Stripes
9. Orion
10. Mustard

Round 5

1. Richard Nixon
2. St Mark
3. Grass
4. Borneo
5. Lactose
6. Rednex
7. Seaweed
8. Macduff
9. Iraq
10. Zirconium

Quiz Thirty Two-Bonus Round Answers

1. Henry I
2. Mine sweeping
3. Garibaldi

Quiz 33

Round 1

1. Who was Vice President under Barack Obama?
2. Which country did Jonah Lomu play rugby for?
3. Which legendary king had a court in Camelot?
4. Who is known in Holland as Zinter Klaus?
5. What title does the vampire have in 'Dracula'?
6. In which US state is Orlando?
7. What is the name of Tony Blair's son born in 2000?
8. Who starred as Ally McBeal?
9. What is the name for an ice hockey pitch?
10. What is the line across the middle of a circle called?

Round 2

1. Which team won the 2014 World Cup of football?
2. What sorts of beans are used in making chocolate?
3. What is the wife of a tsar called?
4. What is the name of Fred Flintstone's pet?
5. What usually gets trapped in a Venus Fly Trap?
6. What is a clavichord?
7. The zodiac sign Pisces covers which two months?
8. In which country would you visit the Francorchamps race track?
9. In which Irish city is the Abbey Theatre?
10. Which cricketer's bat was auctioned for £23000 in 1997?

Round 3

1. What do you fear if you suffer from photophobia?
2. In which US state was George W Bush born?
3. Which group recorded the song 'Children of the Revolution'?
4. What was Zaire renamed in 1997?
5. Which European country is made up of cantons?
6. Hermit and spider are types of what?
7. What was the Spice Girls' first album called?
8. In which sport was Sergei Bubka a world champion?
9. How many times did Queen Elizabeth I marry?
10. What was the first Grand Slam tournament that Roger Federer won without dropping a set?

Round 4

1. How many fortnights are there in two years?
2. What type of weapon is a kukri?
3. In which decade did Apple computers first appear?
4. In CD-ROM, what does the letter R stand for?
5. Which sauce is usually eaten with turkey?
6. The coast of Belgium is on which sea?
7. What two colours make up the flag of Argentina?
8. What is the highest checkout score in a game of 501 in darts?
9. On which river is the city of Adelaide located?
10. How many squares are on a chessboard?

Round 5

1. Which Chappell brothers captained Australia in cricket?
2. In which quiz show is zero the best score?
3. What was the name of the world's first test tube baby?
4. In the first Toy Story, who owns the toys?
5. Where were India's first movie studios?
6. Which version of Windows was launched in 2015?
7. What was the cause of the fire at Windsor Castle in 1992?
8. How is Beethoven's piano sonata No. 14 usually known?
9. What was Michael Jackson's first film?
10. Which company bought You Tube in 2006?

Quiz Thirty Three-Bonus Round Questions

1. In what year was the Mexican Wave first used?
2. Who was the first American to win the Tour de France?
3. What is the drink kumis made from?

Answers Quiz Thirty Three

Round 1

1. Joe Biden
2. New Zealand
3. Arthur
4. Santa Claus
5. Count
6. Florida
7. Leo
8. Calista Flockhart
9. Rink
10. Diameter

Round 2

1. Germany
2. Cocoa beans
3. Tsarina
4. Dino
5. Insects
6. Musical instrument
7. March, April
8. Belgium
9. Dublin
10. Don Bradman's

Round 3

1. Light
2. Connecticut
3. T Rex
4. Congo
5. Switzerland
6. Crab
7. Spice
8. Pole vault
9. None
10. Australian Open 2007

Round 4

1. 52
2. Knife
3. 1970s
4. Read
5. Cranberry
6. North Sea
7. Light blue and white
8. 170
9. River Torrens
10. 64

Round 5

1. Ian and Greg
2. Pointless
3. Louise
4. Andy
5. Bombay/Mumbai
6. Windows 10
7. Electrical fault
8. Moonlight Sonata
9. The Wiz
10. Google

Quiz Thirty Three-Bonus Round Answers

1. 1986
2. Greg Lemond
3. Milk

Quiz 34

Round 1

1. The game of boules is associated with which country?
2. Pisa's leaning tower was built to house what?
3. What did William Tell use to shoot an apple off his son's head?
4. What is the top colour on a rainbow?
5. Who founded Al Qaeda in the late 1980s?
6. Which kitchen item is also a type of drum?
7. Which people used C, D, L and M in their counting system?
8. What are the sides of a stage called?
9. How many wheels does a wheelbarrow usually have?
10. What was Victoria Beckham's maiden name?

Round 2

1. What were the initials of food maker Heinz?
2. What can be a sheet of paper or a part of a plant?
3. In which country is the musical 'Cabaret' set?
4. Queen Nefertiti ruled which country?
5. What does the P stand for in OPEC?
6. In which country is 'The Sound of Music' set?
7. What kind of machine did William Hoover invent?
8. What does kissing the Blarney Stone give you power to do what?
9. What was the profession of Perry Mason?
10. What was the name of Kate Winslet's character in 'Titanic'?

Round 3

1. Which TV series had the character Boss Hogg?
2. The Sargasso Sea is part of which ocean?
3. In which country is the town of Kurri Kurri?
4. Englander is an anagram of which country?
5. The leader of an orchestra plays which instrument?
6. What is at the end of a lacrosse stick?
7. How many beats to the bar are there in basic rock music?
8. What are the US pop charts called?
9. In nautical terms, what is a Blue Peter?
10. What is a flexible diving board called?

Round 4

1. Which Pope died in 2005?
2. In which year did Prince Charles marry Camilla Parker-Bowles?
3. Who is the lead singer of 'Coldplay'?
4. What creature has a name that means idle and lazy?
5. What are dried to make prunes?
6. What are the ends of a magnet called?
7. What is the term for a group of elephants?
8. The moon is said to wax and what else?
9. What colour was the Colonel in 'Cluedo'?
10. What is the introductory page of a website known as?

Round 5

1. Which racing car driver was dubbed 'The Professor of the Track'?
2. What creature can be Golden or Bald?
3. Who was the director of 'Strictly Ballroom'?
4. Who played the title role in the 1953 film 'Houdini'?
5. Which British comedian was Connie Booth married to?
6. What was a gulag in Russia?
7. What words start Psalm 23?
8. What was Muhammad Ali's autobiography called?
9. Which 'N Sync star launched the design label William Rast?
10. How many teams were coached by Australian football coach Mick Malthouse?

Quiz Thirty Four-Bonus Round Questions

1. Which war was ended with the Peace of Vereeniging?
2. What relation was Queen Victoria to George IV?
3. How many books are there in the New Testament?

Answers Quiz Thirty Four

Round 1

1. France
2. Bells
3. Crossbow
4. Red
5. Osama Bin Laden
6. Kettle
7. Romans
8. Wings
9. One
10. Adams

Round 2

1. HJ
2. Leaf
3. Germany
4. Egypt
5. Petroleum
6. Austria
7. Vacuum cleaner
8. Talk
9. Lawyer
10. Rose

Round 3

1. Dukes of Hazzard
2. Atlantic
3. Australia
4. Greenland
5. Violin
6. A net
7. Four
8. Billboard
9. A flag
10. Springboard

Round 4

1. Pope John Paul II
2. 2005
3. Chris Martin
4. Sloth
5. Plums
6. Poles
7. Herd
8. Wane
9. Mustard
10. Home page

Round 5

1. Alain Prost
2. Eagle
3. Baz Luhrmann
4. Tony Curtis
5. John Cleese
6. Prison camp
7. The Lord is my Shepherd
8. The Greatest
9. Justin Timberlake
10. Four

Quiz Thirty Four-Bonus Round Answers

1. Boer War
2. Niece
3. 27

Quiz 35

Round 1

1. What is the name of the Australian music charts?
2. How many French Open titles did Chris Evert win?
3. What shape is a bagel?
4. Who was the director of the 'Lord of the Rings 'movies?
5. Saffron tinges food what colour?
6. What is the second line in a knock-knock joke?
7. Which people first developed central heating?
8. Which country has the most computers?
9. What colour was Queen Elizabeth I's hair?
10. On which instrument might a roll be played?

Round 2

1. Who was the star of 'Nanny McPhee'?
2. What is usually served from a tureen?
3. Which letter is directly below 3 and 4 on a keyboard?
4. What colour is the inside of a coconut?
5. Who wrote the song 'Only the Lonely'?
6. What sport is also a type of shirt?
7. Who had a hit with 'Good Vibrations'?
8. What is a jumbuck?
9. What does the word aloha mean?
10. Who won gold in the 100m in the 1988 Seoul Olympics after Ben Johnson was disqualified?

Round 3

1. Who became World Heavyweight boxing champion in 1987?
2. Australian cricketer Matthew Hayden wrote what sort of book?
3. In Cuba, what is a habanera?
4. Which animal's legs does the Griffin have?
5. What is a puck made from in ice hockey?
6. Which country beginning with E joined the European Union in 2004?
7. Which letter is the symbol for euro currency?
8. Who was Spain's first Formula One world champion?
9. 'A Little Less Conversation' was a hit song for whom?
10. The Bates Motel first appeared in what film?

Round 4

1. How many angles are there on a trapezium?
2. William Hartnell was the first to play which TV character?
3. Which river flows through Belfast?
4. Who thought that everyone would be famous for 15 minutes?
5. Who created 'The Muppets'?
6. Who was the first Queen of England in the 20th century?
7. What is the largest supermarket chain in Australia (as of 2019)?
8. Which South American country did Pope Francis come from?
9. The holiday island of Ibiza belongs to which country?
10. Which famous surfing beach is on the outskirts of Sydney?

Round 5

1. Salina Bay is on which island?
2. What sport is covered in the film 'Million Dollar Baby'?
3. Who played Hercule Poirot in the TV series?
4. At what occasion would you see a returning officer?
5. In which war was the Battle of Bunker Hill?
6. In which country are the Grampians?
7. Who killed the outlaw Billy the Kid?
8. What is controlled by an Emir?
9. What is the name of the family in 'Bob's Burgers'?
10. What are the metal discs on the rim of a tambourine called?

Quiz Thirty Five-Bonus Round Questions

1. Who composed 'The Ring Cycle'?
2. In what year was the QE2 retired from service by Cunard?
3. Who scored a century in the 2007 World Cup cricket Final?

Answers Quiz Thirty Five

Round 1

1. ARIA
2. Seven
3. Round
4. Peter Jackson
5. Yellow
6. Who's there?
7. Romans
8. USA
9. Red
10. Drum

Round 2

1. Emma Thompson
2. Soup/vegetables
3. E
4. White
5. Roy Orbison
6. Polo
7. Beach Boys
8. Sheep
9. Hello or goodbye
10. Carl Lewis

Round 3

1. Mike Tyson
2. Cooking
3. Dance
4. Lion's
5. Rubber
6. Estonia
7. E
8. Fernando Alonso
9. Elvis Presley
10. Psycho

Round 4

1. Four
2. Dr Who
3. Lagan
4. Andy Warhol
5. Jim Henson
6. Queen Victoria
7. Woolworths
8. Argentina
9. Spain
10. Bondi

Round 5

1. Malta
2. Boxing
3. David Suchet
4. An election
5. American War of Independence
6. Australia
7. Pat Garrett
8. An Emirate
9. Belchers
10. Jingles/zils

Quiz Thirty Five-Bonus Round Answers

1. Wagner
2. 2008
3. Adam Gilchrist

Quiz 36

Round 1

1. How many minutes in 11 hours?
2. What does a cactus store inside it?
3. Who was US President on December 31st 1999?
4. Which Beatles song features Father Mackenzie?
5. Who wrote the lyrics for 'Candle in the Wind'?
6. What is the largest lake in the USA?
7. Which TV series was set on Craggy Island?
8. What is a table tennis ball made from?
9. Morphettville racetrack is in which Australian city?
10. What is a moving sheet of ice called?

Round 2

1. What is a meteorite made from?
2. The term fauna refers to what?
3. In which country was tennis player Martina Hingis born?
4. Where can you purchase two items and still have bought lots?
5. Which company launched the PlayStation?
6. Of which country was Bertie Ahern a Prime Minister?
7. Which word describes linking computers together?
8. What colour is pink salmon?
9. In which country was Brigitte Bardot born?
10. For how long were Adolf Hitler and Eva Braun married?

Round 3

1. In which category did Albert Einstein win his Nobel Prize?
2. Which singer became the first to record two James Bond theme tunes?
3. Who was the first Spice Girl to get engaged?
4. Who starred as House in the TV series?
5. On which two countries' borders is Mt Everest?
6. Who had a hit with 'Someone Like You' in 2012?
7. Who is the famous father of singer Norah Jones?
8. Which model was known as 'The Body'?
9. Queens is a borough in which US city?
10. What do you lose if you suffer from alopecia?

Round 4

1. Who wrote 'Go Set a Watchman' in 2015?
2. Who was the first male to claim 13 Grand Slam tennis titles?
3. What type of pet did Sabrina the Teenage Witch have?
4. Which European country has the internet code .hur?
5. Which gridiron team comes from Tampa Bay?
6. By what name is Dr Martin Ellingham better known as?
7. How old was Malcolm Turnbull when he became Australian PM?
8. Which novel features the character Wendy Darling?
9. What is 4 cubed?
10. How many hills of Rome are there?

Round 5

1. In what month did the singer Prince die?
2. Carbs is an abbreviation for which food term?
3. Who became Prime Minister of the United Kingdom in July 2019?
4. What does the V stand for in IVF?
5. Who is Suri Cruise's mother?
6. Which band leader won the first gold disc?
7. A pipistrelle is what kind of creature?
8. What is London's second largest airport?
9. Which river flows through New Orleans?
10. What is Australia's largest bank in terms of assets?

Quiz Thirty Six-Bonus Round Questions

1. Which country was formerly known as Portuguese West Africa?
2. Which Grand Slam title did Jimmy Connors never win?
3. How many wickets did Matthew Hoggard take in the 2006-07 Ashes Series?

Answers Quiz Thirty Six

Round 1

1. 660
2. Water
3. Bill Clinton
4. Eleanor Rigby
5. Bernie Taupin
6. Michigan
7. Father Ted
8. Plastic
9. Adelaide
10. Glacier

Round 2

1. Rock
2. Animals
3. Czechoslovakia
4. An auction
5. Sony
6. Ireland
7. Networking
8. Pink
9. France
10. One day

Round 3

1. Physics
2. Shirley Bassey
3. Posh Spice
4. Hugh Laurie
5. Tibet & Nepal
6. Adele
7. Ravi Shankar
8. Elle Macpherson
9. New York
10. Hair

Round 4

1. Harper Lee
2. Pete Sampras
3. Cat
4. Hungary
5. Buccaneers
6. Doc Martin
7. 60
8. Peter Pan
9. 64
10. Seven

Round 5

1. April
2. Carbohydrates
3. Boris Johnson
4. Vitro
5. Katie Holmes
6. Glenn Miller
7. Bat
8. Gatwick
9. Mississippi
10. Commonwealth Bank of Australia

Quiz Thirty Six-Bonus Round Answers

1. Angola
2. French Open
3. 13

Quiz 37

Round 1

1. Which guitarist had the nickname 'Slowhand'?
2. What was Mary Poppins' job?
3. Who provided the voice of Aslan in the 2005 'Narnia' movie?
4. How many winks describe a nap or short sleep?
5. Status Quo claim their songs are based on how many chords?
6. What was Captain Kidd's first name?
7. Which bird is associated with the drink Guinness?
8. Who is Jayden James Federline's mother?
9. Which US leader had twin daughters Jenna and Barbara?
10. On what date did the devastating tsunami hit South Asia in 2004?

Round 2

1. Where is a fresco painted?
2. 'March of the Volunteers' is the national anthem of which Asian country?
3. Which body of water was known at one time as the German Sea?
4. Who created the character Fred Scuttle?
5. In which US state is the city of Anchorage?
6. Who was elected Lord Mayor of London in 2016?
7. Whose real name was Norma Jean Mortenson?
8. Who was the voice of Garfield in the two movies?
9. How many times did Judy Garland marry?
10. In which decade were camcorders introduced?

Round 3

1. What was David Bowie's real surname?
2. How many operas did Mozart write?
3. What was Star Wars Episode II called?
4. In which city is Penny Lane?
5. Who wrote the sci-fi story, 'I Robot'?
6. In which movie did Gene Kelly roller-skate with Olivia Newton-John?
7. How often does Halley's Comet return?
8. Who covered and charted with the song 'Stairway to Heaven'?
9. During which war was 'Breaker Morant' set?
10. What was the first James Bond film where he asked for his martini to be shaken, not stirred?

Round 4

1. Which country was the first to patent the wine cask?
2. What kind of supernova did Oasis sing about?
3. Who wrote the book 'Hercule Poirot's Christmas?
4. Who is the second voice on 'Do They Know it's Christmas'?
5. In which film did Clint Eastwood say, 'Go ahead, make my day'?
6. The film 'Bird' was about which jazz musician?
7. Where was Gen. Douglas MacArthur when he said 'I shall return'?
8. What type of plane chased Cary Grant in 'North by Northwest'?
9. Which author was known as 'the poet of the dustbowl'?
10. What make of motorcycle did world champion Mick Doohan use?

Round 5

1. 'Sock it to me' became famous on which TV show?
2. Who said the Beatles were more popular than Jesus?
3. What does Charlie Chaplin eat in the film 'The Gold Rush'?
4. How many Von Trapp children are there in 'The Sound of Music?
5. Which country hosted the first Eurovision Song Contest?
6. In which musical did the song 'Memory' feature?
7. In which country is Yellowknife an airport?
8. Uillean pipes are a type of what?
9. Which US President was married to Rosalynn Smith?
10. Which wedding anniversary is linked to tin?

Quiz Thirty Seven-Bonus Round Questions

1. In 1865, where did the Confederate Army surrender?
2. Where is the Masai Mara game reserve?
3. Who was the female leader of the Baader Meinhof terrorist group?

Answers Quiz Thirty Seven

Round 1

1. Eric Clapton
2. Nanny
3. Liam Neeson
4. Forty
5. Three
6. William
7. Toucan
8. Britney Spears
9. George W Bush
10. December 26th

Round 2

1. On a wall
2. China
3. North Sea
4. Benny Hill
5. Alaska
6. Sadiq Khan
7. Marilyn Monroe
8. Bill Murray
9. Five
10. 1980s

Round 3

1. Jones
2. 20
3. Attack of the Clones
4. Liverpool
5. Isaac Asimov
6. Xanadu
7. Every 76 years
8. Rolf Harris
9. Boer War
10. Goldfinger

Round 4

1. Australia
2. Champagne
3. Agatha Christie
4. George Michael
5. Sudden Impact
6. Charlie Parker
7. Australia
8. Crop duster
9. John Steinbeck
10. Honda

Round 5

1. Laugh-In
2. John Lennon
3. His shoe
4. Seven
5. Switzerland
6. Cats
7. Canada
8. Bagpipes
9. Jimmy Carter
10. 10th

Quiz Thirty Seven-Bonus Round Answers

1. Appomattox
2. Kenya
3. Ulrike Meinhof

Quiz 38

Round 1

1. Who drove the fastest milk cart in the west?
2. What were the first flavoured chips in Australia?
3. What REM titled song contains the name of a fruit?
4. What species of bean is Hannibal Lecter fond of?
5. What is the only word uttered in the movie 'Silent Movie'?
6. Who had a hit with the song 'Lost in France'?
7. In what year did the first Paris-Dakar rally take place?
8. Who wrote the 'Da Vinci Code'?
9. Who famously said Australia was on the way to becoming a banana republic?
10. The original Apple logo featured which famous scientist?

Round 2

1. What colour is the border cover of 'National Geographic' magazine?
2. Who wrote the book 'Tropic of Capricorn'?
3. Who wrote the song 'Islands in the Stream'?
4. What is the strait that divides Alaska and Russia?
5. How many of New York's five boroughs do runners pass through in the New York Marathon?
6. Which mountain in NSW holds the Bathurst 1000?
7. Which American said, 'Conceit is God's gift to little men'?
8. What did Leo Fender make?
9. Who won a Grammy in 1992 for 'Tears in Heaven'?
10. Roland Gift was the lead singer of which group?

Round 3

1. Hopkins airport is in which US state?
2. In what year was AIDS officially recognised?
3. The Angelina Jolie Movie 'A Mighty Heart' is set in which country?
4. Joe Elliott was a vocalist with which heavy metal band?
5. In which decade of the 20th century did author HG Wells die?
6. What is the traditional gift for a 13th wedding anniversary?
7. Which member of the Beatles was nicknamed 'The Dark Horse'?
8. Which US President said 'Read my lips-no new taxes'?
9. Which member of 'Kiss' is known for his lengthy tongue?
10. Which medical TV series is named after a medical textbook?

Round 4

1. What does singer Pink have tattooed on the back of her neck?
2. What does the Q stand for in the James Bond character?
3. Who is the lead singer of the Beach Boys?
4. In what country was Scrooge McDuck born?
5. The song Money is on which Pink Floyd album?
6. Who won the men's singles title at Wimbledon in 1987?
7. In comics, who is the world's richest boy?
8. PayPal is a subsidiary of what?
9. Which of the Muppets was fond of biscuits?
10. Who wrote the book 'Chitty, Chitty Bang, Bang?

Round 5

1. Which musical was based on the life of Eva Peron?
2. What nationality was oceanographer Jacques Cousteau?
3. Which of the Thunderbirds looked after underwater rescues?
4. Which pop group was in Africa in 1983?
5. Who was the lead actress in the movie 'The Ring'?
6. What is the value of a US 'greenback'?
7. What does GDP stand for?
8. Who is the highest earning British author?
9. Who recorded the album 'Transformer'?
10. With whom did David Bowie record 'Under Pressure'?

Quiz Thirty Eight-Bonus Round Questions

1. How many Formula One wins did Michael Schumacher have?
2. In which century was the Bank of England founded?
3. What was the previous name of Belarus?

Answers Quiz Thirty Eight

Round 1

1. Ernie
2. Cheese and onion
3. Orange crush
4. Fava
5. Non
6. Bonnie Tyler
7. 1978
8. Dan Brown
9. Paul Keating
10. Isaac Newton

Round 2

1. Yellow
2. Henry Miller
3. Barry Gibb
4. Bering Strait
5. All of them
6. Mt Panorama
7. Harry S Truman
8. Guitars
9. Eric Clapton
10. Fine Young Cannibals

Round 3

1. Ohio
2. 1981
3. Pakistan
4. Def Leppard
5. 1940s
6. Pearls
7. George Harrison
8. George HW Bush
9. Gene Simmons
10. Grey's Anatomy

Round 1

1. A barcode
2. Quartermaster
3. Mike Love
4. Scotland
5. Dark Side of the Moon
6. Pat Cash
7. Richie Rich
8. eBay
9. Cookie Monster
10. Ian Fleming

Round 2

1. Evita
2. French
3. Thunderbird 4
4. Toto
5. Naomi Watts
6. A dollar
7. Gross Domestic Product
8. JK Rowling
9. Lou Reed
10. Queen

Quiz Thirty Eight-Bonus Round Answers

1. 91
2. 17th Century
3. Belorussia

Quiz 39

Round 1

1. In which city are the Australian rugby league team the Broncos based?
2. What was the name of Tonto's horse?
3. What famous song was about a three-legged man?
4. What relation to James Bond did Woody Allen play?
5. In the song Love Shack, how big was their Chrysler?
6. What was the movie spin-off of the TV series 'The Munsters'?
7. Which Irish band released the song 'Zombie'?
8. Whose life was featured in 'The Boy from Oz'?
9. What book was a follow up to 'Jaws'?
10. On what day does the Sydney to Hobart Yacht Race start?

Round 2

1. Which singer was Kung Fu Fighting in 1974?
2. Who has won four Best Director Academy Awards?
3. Where was the Exxon Valdez oil spill in 1989?
4. Whose father was a geography teacher in Willie Wonka & the Chocolate Factory?
5. What is the home of the Phantom called?
6. Which AFL team is referred to as the Purple Haze?
7. Which member of the Brady Bunch needed glasses?
8. In which decade was the Itty Bitty Book Light invented?
9. Who did Roger Federer beat to win the 2017 Australian Open?
10. What is the final line in 'Gone with the Wind'?

Round 3

1. What event is first in the decathlon?
2. What are calderas?
3. How did Emiliano Zapata, the Mexican revolutionary die?
4. What is a folded pizza called?
5. Where is Marsala, famed for its fortified wine?
6. In Fahrenheit, at what temperature does paper burn?
7. Who directed 'No Country for Old Men'?
8. In which country did the game snakes and ladders originate?
9. How many points would the word science score in Scrabble?
10. Who teaches potions at Hogwarts?

Round 4

1. Professor Weirdo created which cartoon character?
2. What is the name of the Phantom's horse?
3. In comics, what did the original DC stand for?
4. What was the name and number of the computer in 2001: A Space Odyssey?
5. In which decade was the electric toothbrush invented?
6. What is another name for a cochlear?
7. What was the first album pressed on CD in Australia?
8. What operating system followed Windows XP?
9. Relating to electronic devices, what is 'App' short for?
10. Who starred in the 2002 film 'The Time Machine'?

Round 5

1. Which US President said, 'We must use time as a tool, not as a couch?
2. Which soap opera uses an hourglass in its opening titles?
3. Who had a hit with 'Midnight at the Oasis'?
4. What optical aid was invented by Benjamin Franklin?
5. Shogi is a Japanese form of which game?
6. How many fingers did Anne Boleyn have?
7. What part of the body is studied by a mycologist?
8. Who is older-Joan Collins or Michael Caine?
9. What sort of creature is a killdeer?
10. Who was the youngest General in the American Civil War?

Quiz Thirty Nine-Bonus Round Questions

1. How many romance novels did Barbara Cartland write?
2. In what year was Queen Victoria born?
3. What Australian film was the first to be shot in colour?

Answers Quiz Thirty Nine

Round 1

1. Brisbane
2. Scout
3. Jake the Peg
4. Nephew
5. As big as a whale
6. Munster Go Home
7. The Cranberries
8. Peter Allen's
9. The Deep
10. December 26th

Round 2

1. Carl Douglas
2. John Ford
3. Prince William Sound
4. Mike Teavee's
5. Skull Cave
6. Fremantle Dockers
7. Jan Brady
8. 1970s
9. Rafael Nadal
10. Tomorrow is another Day

Round 3

1. 100m
2. Volcanic craters
3. Assassinated
4. Calzone
5. Sicily
6. Fahrenheit 451
7. Joel & Ethan Cohen
8. India
9. 50
10. Severus Snape

Round 4

1. Milton the Monster
2. Hero
3. Detective comics
4. HAL 9000
5. 1950s
6. Bionic ear
7. Whispering Jack
8. Windows Vista
9. Application
10. Guy Pearce

Round 5

1. John F Kennedy
2. Days of our Lives
3. Maria Muldaur
4. Bifocal lenses
5. Chess
6. Eleven
7. Muscles
8. Michael Caine
9. A bird
10. George A Custer

Quiz Thirty Nine-Bonus Round Answers

1. 723
2. 1819
3. Jedda

Quiz 40

Round 1

1. In which country did Lego originate?
2. By what name was GI Joe marketed in England?
3. Who had a hit in 1979 with the song Cars?
4. Who played Popeye the sailor in the 1980 film?
5. In Beany and Cecil, what kind of creature was Cecil?
6. What did President Lyndon B Johnson declare war on in 1964?
7. Who narrated the TV series 'World at War'?
8. How was Bulgarian dissident writer Georgi Markov assassinated?
9. Which sportsman was Australian of the Year in 2004?
10. Which company did George Jetson work for?

Round 2

1. What was the nickname for English cricketer Frank Tyson?
2. What was Harry Casey's band better known as?
3. In which decade did the weather Channel begin in the US?
4. Snow Patrol had a massive hit with which song?
5. Who was Maxwell Smart's best man when he and '99' got married?
6. What percentage of marriages in Australia ends in divorce?
7. In which decade did Batman appear in comic book form?
8. Which 'A Christmas Carol' character shares a name with a 1960s pop star?
9. In what city was the TV series Cagney & Lacey set?
10. On which Isle is Parkhurst Prison?

Round 3

1. How many times did Ivan Lendl win Wimbledon?
2. What is the name given to a young deer?
3. What colour are the pockets on a roulette wheel?
4. In what year did Whitney Houston die?
5. Which London Park is also the name of a colour?
6. What was Robin's true identity in the Batman TV series?
7. In what decade was the drink Milo developed in Sydney Australia?
8. Which Christmas song opens the first Die Hard film?
9. What occupation did Clint Eastwood have in 'Play Misty for Me'?
10. What is regarded as Australia's first martial arts film?

Round 4

1. In what year of the 1960s was the famous Elvis 'Comeback' special?
2. Which film had the line 'What we've got here is a failure to communicate'?
3. In what year did Margaret Thatcher become British PM?
4. Irishman Michael Fagan broke into whose bedroom in 1982?
5. Which American President said 'I am not a crook'?
6. What was Scooby Doo's favourite food?
7. The Da Vinci Code film opens with a murder at which Paris landmark?
8. Who played Gilbert Grape in 'What's Eating Gilbert Grape'?
9. Who wrote 'Around the World in Eighty Days'?
10. Which group had the song 'A Town like Alice'?

Round 5

1. The horse Seabiscuit raced in which decade?
2. How many bones does a baby have when it is born?
3. Which James Bond star has the middle name Wroughton?
4. Actor Omar Sharif was a highly ranked what type of card player?
5. How many times is the word money mentioned in the ABBA song, Money, Money, Money?
6. What's the Frequency Kenneth? Is from which REM album?
7. Topol was famous for playing the lead in which musical?
8. Which Beatle's son had a hit with Saltwater in 1991?
9. Which song had the line 'I get knocked down, but I get up again?
10. In 1992, which actor did one handed push ups at the Academy Awards?

Quiz Forty-Bonus Round Questions

1. How tall was singer Prince?
2. Which country was the top producer of kiwifruit in 2007?
3. Which English football manager said, 'I wouldn't say I was the best manager in the business, but I was in the top one'?

Answers Quiz Forty

Round 1

1. Denmark
2. Action Man
3. Gary Numan
4. Robin Williams
5. Sea serpent
6. Poverty
7. Laurence Olivier
8. Poison tipped umbrella
9. Steve Waugh
10. Spacely Space Sprockets Inc.

Round 2

1. Typhoon
2. KC & Sunshine Band
3. 1980s
4. Chasing Cars
5. The Admiral
6. 40%
7. 1930s
8. Tiny Tim
9. New York
10. Isle of Wight

Round 3

1. None
2. Fawn
3. Red, black, green (0)
4. 2012
5. Green
6. Dick Grayson
7. 1930s
8. Jingle Bell Rock
9. Disc jockey
10. The Man from Hong Kong

Round 4

1. 1968
2. Cool Hand Luke
3. 1979
4. The Queen's
5. Richard Nixon
6. Scooby snacks
7. Louvre
8. Johnny Depp
9. Jules Verne
10. The Jam

Round 5

1. 1930s
2. 300
3. Daniel Craig
4. Bridge
5. Twenty one times
6. Monster
7. Fiddler on the Roof
8. John Lennon's
9. Tubthumping
10. Jack Palance

Quiz Forty-Bonus Round Answers

1. 157 cm/5.15 ft
2. Italy
3. Brian Clough

Quiz 41

Round 1

1. Who wrote the book Jurassic Park?
2. Who had a hit with the song 'Sunshine Superman'?
3. What primary gas is used to inflate the airbags in cars?
4. Which song is longer in running time-American Pie or Stairway to Heaven?
5. What planet do the Transformers come from?
6. In which decade did the bullet trains begin operation in Japan?
7. What was the first name of cartoon character Mr Magoo?
8. What is the name of the ship's computer in Red Dwarf?
9. In what sport was Australian Geoff Hunt a world champion?
10. Who played General George S Patton in the movie Patton?

Round 2

1. What type of wedding did Billy Idol sing about?
2. Who composed the soundtrack for Rabbit Proof Fence?
3. Which 1988 film starring Kurt Russell shares its name with a cocktail?
4. Which Apollo mission became the first to orbit the moon in 1968?
5. Who played alongside Clint Eastwood in Thunderbolt and Lightfoot?
6. In which years did the Spice Girls have their comeback tour?
7. Which British band released the album Communiqué in 1979?
8. Who created the detective Mike Hammer?
9. Former British PM Margaret Thatcher was once referred to as Attila the what?
10. Which book by Roald Dahl features the characters called Cloud Men?

Round 3

1. 'Super-Size Me' was a documentary about eating which fast food exclusively for a month?
2. Who was the youngest ever man to win the French Open in 1989?
3. In the TV series 'The O C' what do the letters O and C stand for?
4. Which mountain erupted in the USA in 1980?
5. What size shoe was worn by Ian Thorpe on the show Undercover Angels?
6. Which Simpson's character has the catchphrase 'haw, haw!'?
7. Which title is given to the wife of a Duke?
8. Which is the longest river in the UK?
9. Which precious metal has the chemical symbol Pd?
10. The 'Maigret' novels were written by which author?

Round 4

1. Montmartre is a large hill in which French city?
2. Which river runs through Newcastle (UK) city centre?
3. What is the typical par score on a championship golf course?
4. Complete the proverb, 'No man is a...' what?
5. What was the occupation of Mr Creevey in the Harry Potter book series?
6. What is the name of the freeware web browser developed by Google?
7. Which country has the greater population, Ethiopia or Pakistan?
8. Thirty-six percent of all soy beans are produced in which country?
9. Yuri Gagarin was the first man to orbit the earth. What was the name of his spacecraft?
10. What is more commonly referred to as Dry Ice?

Round 5

1. What Atomic number does the element Helium have?
2. Which playwright wrote Waiting for Godot?
3. How many dots are there on five dice?
4. Of which Latin term is 'e.g.' an abbreviation?
5. Which letter sits farthest to the right on a QWERTY keyboard?
6. Which actor appeared in the most 'Carry On' films?
7. Of what is herpetology the study?
8. Who was the patron saint of animals?
9. In how many films did Sean Connery play James Bond?
10. What were the first names of the crime writer P.D. James?

Quiz Forty One-Bonus Round Questions

1. Which Darts player hit the first ever televised nine-dart finish?
2. In which year did the Romans invade Britain?
3. What nationality is the satellite navigation and mapping company TomTom?

Answers Quiz Forty One

Round 1

1. Michael Crichton
2. Donovan
3. Nitrogen
4. American Pie
5. Cybertron
6. 1960s
7. Quincy
8. Holly
9. Squash
10. George C Scott

Round 2

1. White wedding
2. Peter Gabriel
3. Tequila Sunrise
4. Apollo 8
5. Jeff Bridges
6. 2007-2008
7. Dire Straits
8. Mickey Spillane
9. Hen
10. James and the Giant Peach

Round 3

1. McDonald's
2. Michael Chang
3. Orange County
4. Mt St Helens
5. Size 17
6. Nelson Mutz
7. Duchess
8. River Severn
9. Palladium
10. Georges Simenon

Round 4

1. Paris
2. River Tyne
3. 72
4. Island
5. Milkman
6. Google Chrome
7. Pakistan
8. United States
9. Vostok I
10. Solid carbon dioxide

Round 5

1. 2
2. Samuel Beckett
3. 105
4. Exempli Gratia
5. P
6. Kenneth Williams
7. Amphibians and reptiles
8. St Francis of Assisi
9. Seven
10. Phyllis Dorothy

Quiz Forty One-Bonus Round Answers

1. John Lowe
2. 55 B.C
3. Dutch

Quiz 42

Round 1

1. What is the surname of Raymond in the US television show 'Everybody Loves Raymond'?
2. A megaton is the equivalent of how many tons of TNT?
3. What is the title of the shortest novel by Charles Dickens?
4. The US animated television series 'Family Guy' is set in a fictional city in which state?
5. During which month in 1937 was the Golden Gate Bridge in California officially opened?
6. Prairie Wolf is another name for which animal?
7. Mount Aconcagua is in which South American country?
8. Which animal represents the deadly sin of envy?
9. The German word Reich means what?
10. Myocardial infarction is better known as what?

Round 2

1. In the movie industry what are the Gaffer, Best boy, and Key grip responsible for?
2. What is the biggest-selling album in history?
3. How many finger holes does a recorder have running down the front?
4. Which island does Japan's capital city Tokyo belong to?
5. Who provides the voice of Stewie Griffin in the TV series Family Guy?
6. Which of Snow White's dwarfs has the longest name?
7. The River Amstel flows through which European capital city?
8. What year was the first iPhone (iPhone 2G) released?
9. Who was the leader of Germany during the First World War?
10. What are the colours on an Aldi store?

Round 3

1. Which body organ produces bile?
2. Which land snake has the most toxic venom in the world?
3. On which river did a pilot named Sully make an emergency landing in 2009?
4. Which film series stars Mark Wahlberg and the voice of Seth MacFarlane?
5. What was the title of George Michael's first solo single?
6. Which 2015 movie features a song called 'Writing's on the Wall' by Sam Smith?
7. Which solar system planet experiences the hottest surface temperature?
8. What type of animals make up the biggest group of amphibians?
9. Which is the closest prime number to 100?
10. How many squares are there on a standard Scrabble board?

Round 4

1. Which chemical element has the atomic number three?
2. How many different animals are there in the Chinese Zodiac?
3. 'The Laughing Cavalier' is a 1624 Baroque portrait by which Dutch painter?
4. Which has the greater land mass, North Korea or South Korea?
5. What is the capital of Lebanon?
6. What is the official language of Andorra?
7. 'Thicken' is an anagram of which other word?
8. To which country do the Faroe Islands belong?
9. In February 2017 Queen Elizabeth II became the first British monarch to reach which jubilee?
10. What is the name of Ben Affleck's younger brother, also an actor?

Round 5

1. How many long triangles are there in total on a backgammon board?
2. How many permanently inhabited Channel Islands are there?
3. Which letter in Morse code consists of one single dash?
4. The loganberry is a hybrid of which two fruits?
5. A 'Harvey Wallbanger' is a cocktail consisting of vodka, orange juice and what?
6. How often does a 'vicennial' event occur?
7. What is the national flower of Scotland?
8. What were the first names of detectives Dalziel and Pascoe?
9. What was the name of the first Roald Dahl children's book to be published?
10. Aegean Airlines is the largest airline of which country?

Quiz Forty Two-Bonus Round Questions

1. According to Guinness World Records Jeanne Louise Calment of France holds the record for being the oldest human being to have ever lived (fully authenticated). To what age did she survive?
2. Who produced a series of oil paintings in 1943 known as the 'Four Freedoms'?
3. Italian Antonio Stradivari produced how many violins?

Answers Quiz Forty Two

Round 1

1. Barone
2. One million
3. Hard Times
4. Rhode Island
5. May
6. Coyote
7. Argentina
8. Snake
9. Empire
10. Heart attack

Round 2

1. Lighting
2. Thriller-Michael Jackson
3. Seven
4. Honshu
5. Seth MacFarlane
6. Bashful
7. Amsterdam
8. 2007
9. Wilhelm II
10. Red, blue, yellow, orange, white

Round 3

1. Liver
2. Inland taipan
3. Hudson River
4. Ted
5. Careless Whisper
6. Spectre
7. Venus
8. Frogs
9. 101
10. 225

Round 4

1. Lithium
2. 12
3. Frans Hal
4. North Korea
5. Beirut
6. Catalan
7. Kitchen
8. Denmark
9. Sapphire
10. Casey Affleck

Round 5

1. 24
2. 8
3. T
4. Raspberry and blackberry
5. Galliano
6. Once every 20 years
7. Thistle
8. Andy Dalziel and Peter Pascoe
9. The Gremlins
10. Greece

Quiz Forty Two-Bonus Round Answers

1. 122
2. Norman Rockwell
3. 960

Quiz 43

Round 1

1. Which two months of the year are named after Roman Emperors?
2. Geert Wilders is a right wing politician in which country?
3. What is the term on Wikipedia for a short article in need of expansion?
4. Kimberlite is an igneous rock mined because it contains what?
5. What does the song title 'O sole mio' mean?
6. What is the logo of the website Wikileaks?
7. What is the 4th largest island in the world?
8. What does a fletcher specialise in making?
9. How many gold medals did Mo Farah win at the 2016 Summer Olympics?
10. What are pince-nez?

Round 2

1. Coven is the collective name for a group of what?
2. Which body organ is affected by glaucoma?
3. Raymond Reddington features as a lead character in which American thriller series?
4. Who famously said, "Dr Livingstone, I presume?"
5. Which sport is associated with Olympic gold medallist Ryan Lochte?
6. How many degrees do the interior angles of a triangle always equal?
7. How many countries of the world begin with the letter Z?
8. Maundy Thursday commemorates which event?
9. What name was given to the cup from which Jesus drank from at the Last Supper?
10. Which river flows through Glasgow?

Round 3

1. Who was Chief Inspector George Gently's sidekick?
2. Where is Sir Isaac Newton buried?
3. Which Hindu God is responsible for creation of the world and all its creatures?
4. What is the capital of Cyprus?
5. According the proverb, who is not recognised in his own land?
6. Who is the leader of North Korea? (as of 2020)
7. Which country has a national anthem entitled 'Wilhelmus'?
8. What is 2017 in Roman numerals
9. How many rooms are there in the original version of the game of 'Cluedo'?
10. How is the condition 'scrivener's palsy' better known as?

Round 4

1. Who is the Prime Minister of Great Britain? (as of 2020)
2. Which movie won Best Film at the 2017 Academy Awards?
3. Narendra Modi is the Prime Minister of which country?
4. Which city lost the right to host the 2022 Commonwealth Games?
5. What is the capital of New Zealand?
6. In what year was Darwin bombed by Japanese planes?
7. What is myopia?
8. One and a half litres of champagne is known as a what?
9. What instrument has been nicknamed the 'Mississippi Saxophone'?
10. How many sides does an icosagon have?

Round 5

1. Where in London is there a bronze statue of Charlie Chaplin?
2. What is the real surname of Sting from The Police?
3. What creature appears on the flag of Wales?
4. What animal is associated with the beginning of an MGM film?
5. What is the highest mountain in the Karakorum Range of mountains?
6. If you suffer from 'gymnophobia', what are you most afraid of?
7. Who famously stated that'... an army marches on its stomach'?
8. In nature, how many arms (or legs) does a starfish have?
9. How many seats did the spitfire fighter plane have?
10. If you see FCUK on a t-shirt, what does the FC stand for?

Quiz Forty Three-Bonus Round Questions

1. How many Academy Award nominations did Katharine Hepburn receive?
2. Which kinds of bulbs were once exchanged as a form of currency?
3. How many tales are told in the Canterbury Tales?

Answers Quiz Forty Three

Round 1

1. July, August
2. Holland
3. Stub
4. Diamonds
5. My sunshine
6. Spectacles
7. Madagascar
8. Arrows
9. Two
10. A pair of glasses with a nose piece

Round 2

1. Witches
2. Eyes
3. The Blacklist
4. Sir Henry Morton Stanley
5. Swimming
6. 180
7. Two-Zambia, Zimbabwe
8. The Last Supper
9. Holy Grail
10. River Clyde

Round 3

1. John Bacchus
2. Westminster Abbey
3. Brahma
4. Nicosia
5. A prophet
6. Kim Jong-un
7. Holland
8. MMXVII
9. Nine
10. Writer's cramp

Round 4

1. Boris Johnson
2. Moonlight
3. India
4. Durban
5. Wellington
6. 1942
7. Short sightedness
8. Magnum
9. Harmonica
10. 20

Round 5

1. Leicester Square
2. Summer
3. Dragon
4. Lion
5. K2
6. Nudity
7. Napoleon Bonaparte
8. Five
9. One
10. French Connection

Quiz Forty Three-Bonus Round Answers

1. 12
2. Tulips
3. 24

Quiz 44

Round 1

1. Magyar is the official language of which country?
2. George I was the first king of which royal house?
3. Who was the supreme commander of the D-Day invasion?
4. Which actress was 'America's Sweetheart'?
5. Who won five of the first eight Formula 1 World Championships?
6. Which singer created the alter ego Aladdin Sane?
7. Who wrote the book 'A Brief History of Time'?
8. What is a type of font and a hall in a Sherlock Holmes story?
9. What is the capital of Saudi Arabia?
10. In the Bible, who was the brother of Moses?

Round 2

1. On which island is the ruined palace of Knossos?
2. Who was crowned King of Scotland in 1306?
3. The peninsula of Jutland lies mainly in which country?
4. What was the name of the black panther in 'The Jungle Book'?
5. How many sides does a heptagon have?
6. In how many parts is Shakespeare's Henry VI?
7. Who in Australian politics was 'The Little Digger'?
8. The sangha is the monastic order in which religion?
9. What four words follow 'To be or not to be' from Hamlet?
10. Who tells the tales of 1001 Nights?

Round 3

1. Who played Mrs Robinson in the film 'The Graduate'?
2. Who wrote and directed the film 'Love Actually'?
3. Where in the Solar System can the Cassini Division be found?
4. How many playing pieces are there in a game of backgammon?
5. Who sang the title song of the James Bond film, 'You Only Live Twice'?
6. Who played Ron Weasley in the Harry Potter films?
7. Where would a toque be worn?
8. Which element is deadly to Superman?
9. What is the national airline of Australia?
10. Who gave Excalibur to King Arthur?

Round 4

1. Which fruit is known as the love apple?
2. A faucet is an American word for what item?
3. The Pilkington Company is best known for which product?
4. Tallinn is the capital city of which European country?
5. Bibendum is the name of which famous advertising logo?
6. Carol I and Carol II were monarchs of which European country?
7. Who was the Roman God of war?
8. What nut is used to make marzipan?
9. Andre Rieu is a popular performer of which instrument?
10. Steinlager beer comes from which country?

Round 5

1. Who played Baldrick in the 'Blackadder TV series?
2. Which US President owned a cat named Socks?
3. What is the capital of Western Australia?
4. What is hit by a racket in the game of badminton?
5. Dry ice is a solid form of what?
6. What was the surname of the WWI flying ace the Red Baron?
7. In which US state is the city of Chicago?
8. What was founded by William Booth in 1865?
9. Which building will supposedly fall if the ravens leave?
10. Which band had a hit with 'Rock the Casbah'?

Quiz Forty Four-Bonus Round Questions

1. Oil of vitriol is another name for which acid?
2. In which three James Bond films does Shirley Bassey sing the theme song?
3. What was the first album released by Virgin Records?

Answers Quiz Forty Four

Round 1

1. Hungary
2. Hanover
3. Dwight D Eisenhower
4. Mary Pickford
5. Juan Manuel Fangio
6. David Bowie
7. Stephen Hawking
8. Baskerville
9. Riyadh
10. Aaron

Round 2

1. Crete
2. Robert the Bruce
3. Denmark
4. Bagheera
5. Seven
6. Three
7. Billy Hughes
8. Buddhism
9. That is the question
10. Scheherazade

Round 3

1. Anne Bancroft
2. Richard Curtis
3. Rings of Saturn
4. 30
5. Nancy Sinatra
6. Rupert Grint
7. On the head
8. Kryptonite
9. QANTAS
10. The Lady of the Lake-Viviane

Round 4

1. Tomato
2. Tap
3. Glass
4. Estonia
5. Michelin Man
6. Romania
7. Mars
8. Almond
9. Violin
10. New Zealand

Round 5

1. Tony Robinson
2. Bill Clinton
3. Perth
4. Shuttlecock
5. Carbon dioxide
6. Von Richthofen
7. Illinois
8. Salvation Army
9. Tower of London
10. The Clash

Quiz Forty Four-Bonus Round Answers

1. Sulphuric Acid
2. Goldfinger, Diamonds are Forever, Moonraker
3. Tubular Bells

Quiz 45

Round 1

1. Which state of Australia is known as the Festival State?
2. Which desert lies in Sudan between the River Nile and the Red Sea?
3. What colour is Thomas the Tank Engine?
4. If Polly put the kettle on, who took it off again?
5. Which Premier league team were originally known as Ardwick FC?
6. In computing, what is the word blog short for?
7. What is the currency of Bolivia?
8. On which ship did Fletcher Christian lead the mutiny?
9. Which dynasty ruled China from 1368 to 1644?
10. What was the only novel written by Oscar Wilde?

Round 2

1. Which airline carries a maple leaf design on their tailfin?
2. The sorceress Medea was the wife of which Greek hero?
3. Which singer has a backing band called the Bad Seeds?
4. What is a solid shape with 12 faces called?
5. In bingo what number relates to the word legs?
6. Which South American country is the only former British colony?
7. Which card game uses a wooden peg board for scoring?
8. Who became lead singer of Genesis in 1975?
9. Which drink takes its name from the Gaelic for 'water of life'?
10. What is dendrophobia a fear of?

Round 3

1. Which of the United States is the most southerly?
2. A rollmop is a food dish comprising which fish?
3. The Weather Girls had a hit in 1983 with which song?
4. The line 'I am serious and don't call me Shirley' is from which film?
5. Who founded the Mormons in 1830?
6. Who wrote 'The Name of the Rose'?
7. In which city did the St Valentine's Day Massacre take place?
8. The Pahlavi Dynasty ruled which country from 1925 to 1979?
9. Which strait separates Australia and Papua New Guinea?
10. Ilya Kuryakin was a character in which TV series?

Round 4

1. What is the capital of Vietnam?
2. What type of instrument is a bodhran?
3. How many pairs of chromosomes does a human cell have?
4. On which river is the Hoover Dam?
5. In music, a quaver is half as long as which note?
6. What was prohibited by the 18th Amendment in the USA?
7. Where would you find the Lake of Death and the Sea of Geniuses?
8. Which king of England went to the Third Crusade?
9. What did Wilhelm von Rontgen discover in 1895?
10. Which Australian rugby league team is nicknamed the Bunnies?

Round 5

1. Which Rolls-Royce model was produced between 1906 and 1925?
2. In which novel is Newspeak the official language?
3. Arctophilists collect which children's toy?
4. Helen Porter Mitchell was the real name for which Australian opera singer?
5. The Simplon railway tunnel is between which two countries?
6. Who is the originator of the concept of lateral thinking?
7. What item of clothing is called pants by Americans?
8. What cricket score is considered bad luck by Australians?
9. In which year was the Cuban Missile Crisis?
10. A-Ha provided the theme song for which James Bond film?

Quiz Forty Five-Bonus Round Questions

1. Who was the last Holy Roman Emperor?
2. In what year was Virgin Records founded by Richard Branson?
3. In which country do 100 Tiyn make a Tenge?

Answers Quiz Forty Five

Round 1

1. South Australia
2. Nubian Desert
3. Blue
4. Sukey
5. Manchester City
6. Web log
7. Boliviano
8. Bounty
9. Ming Dynasty
10. The Picture of Dorian Gray

Round 2

1. Air Canada
2. Jason
3. Nick Cave
4. Dodecahedron
5. Eleven
6. Guyana
7. Cribbage
8. Phil Collins
9. Whiskey
10. Trees

Round 3

1. Hawaii
2. Herring
3. It's Raining Men
4. Airplane/Flying High
5. Joseph Smith Jr
6. Umberto Eco
7. Chicago
8. Iran/Persia
9. Torres Strait
10. The Man from U.N.C.L.E.

Round 4

1. Hanoi
2. Small Irish drum
3. 23
4. Colorado
5. Crochet
6. Sale of alcohol
7. On the moon
8. Richard the Lionheart
9. X-Rays
10. South Sydney

Round 5

1. Silver Ghost
2. 1984
3. Teddy bear
4. Dame Nellie Melba
5. Switzerland and Italy
6. Edward de Bono
7. Trousers
8. 87
9. 1962
10. The Living Daylights

Quiz Forty Five-Bonus Round Answers

1. Francis II
2. 1970
3. Kazakhstan

Quiz 46

Round 1

1. On which island is the Indonesian capital Jakarta?
2. Which toy takes its name from the Danish for 'play well'?
3. What mineral is crucial for healthy bones and teeth?
4. What is the capital of the US state Louisiana?
5. How should a musical piece marked 'adagio' be played?
6. What flower shares its name with part of the human eye?
7. Which country's flag has five crosses of St George on it?
8. Bombay and London are types of which spirit?
9. In which European country is Lake Ladoga?
10. Which horror film star was born William Pratt?

Round 2

1. What event started the French Revolution in 1789?
2. On which mountain did Moses receive the Ten Commandments?
3. Who was the Greek goddess of retribution?
4. Who was Harry Potter's godfather?
5. Mehmed VI was the last Sultan of which empire?
6. Who directed the films Gandhi and Chaplin?
7. What type of creature was Mrs Tiggy-Winkle?
8. The Bushmen are native to which desert?
9. Who composed the Liberty Bell March?
10. Which cricket reference book was first published in 1864?

Round 3

1. Who shot Jesse James?
2. What is notable about John Cage's composition of 4'33'?
3. In which TV series will you find Bitzer the dog?
4. What breed of dog was Rin Tin Tin?
5. Which Portuguese striker won the Golden Boot at the 1966 World Cup?
6. The Australian health education programme 'Slip, slop, slap' started in what year of the 1980s?
7. Which fish shares its name with a popular hairstyle in the 1980s?
8. What is Europe's second longest mountain range?
9. Which river enters the Indian Ocean at Fremantle?
10. Who wrote the 1812 Overture?

Round 4

1. What species is the symbol of the World Wildlife Fund for nature?
2. Dale Arden was the girlfriend of which hero?
3. In snooker which ball is worth five points?
4. Which animals live in setts?
5. The March of the Toreadors appears in which opera?
6. In which city is the TV series Cheers set?
7. Which king is murdered by Macbeth?
8. For which film did Clark Gable receive a Best Actor Oscar?
9. Which breakfast cereal was marketed by Tony the Tiger?
10. Which guitarist's real name was James Marshall?

Round 5

1. Who was Prime Minister of Australia in the 1950s?
2. What term is given to a group of two or more atoms bonded together?
3. Alphabetically, what is the last sign of the zodiac?
4. With which children's programme is 'Can we fix it? associated?
5. Which Beatles song begins with 'In the town where I was born'?
6. How many times was Pierre Trudeau Prime Minister of Canada?
7. Which company makes the Firefox internet browser?
8. What is the tallest breed of dog?
9. Washington DC stands on which river?
10. What term is given to theatres in New York with less than 100 seats?

Quiz Forty Six-Bonus Round Questions

1. Which two countries entered the EU at the same time as the UK in 1973?
2. Eboracum is the Roman name for which English city?
3. In what year was the Pulitzer Prize first awarded?

Answers Quiz Forty Six

Round 1

1. Java
2. Lego
3. Calcium
4. Baton Rouge
5. Slowly
6. Iris
7. Georgia
8. Gin
9. Russia
10. Boris Karloff

Round 2

1. Storming the Bastille
2. Mt Sinai
3. Nemesis
4. Sirius Black
5. Ottoman Empire
6. Richard Attenborough
7. A hedgehog
8. Kalahari
9. John Philip Sousa
10. Wisden Cricket Almanack

Round 3

1. Robert Ford
2. It is completely silent
3. Shaun the Sheep
4. German shepherd
5. Eusebio
6. 1981
7. Mullet
8. Carpathians
9. Swan River
10. Tchaikovsky

Round 4

1. Giant panda
2. Flash Gordon
3. Blue
4. Badgers
5. Carmen
6. Boston
7. Duncan
8. It Happened One Night
9. Kellogg's Frosties
10. Jimi Hendrix

Round 5

1. Robert Menzies
2. Molecule
3. Virgo
4. Bob the Builder
5. Yellow Submarine
6. Two
7. Mozilla
8. Irish wolfhound
9. Potomac
10. Off-off Broadway

Quiz Forty Six-Bonus Round Answers

1. Denmark & Republic of Ireland
2. York
3. 1917

Quiz 47

Round 1

1. Which jazz musician was nicknamed 'Satchmo'?
2. What is the sum of the interior angles of a pentagon?
3. What is the sacred flower of the Buddhist religion?
4. Which band did Dave Grohl found after Nirvana?
5. In which US city is the Watergate building?
6. Which country is entirely surrounded by South Africa?
7. Which song has the opening line 'Starry, starry night'?
8. Which barbarian warlord died of a nosebleed on his wedding night?
9. Who was the comedy partner of Bud Abbott?
10. Who led a protest march against a salt tax in India in 1930?

Round 2

1. Gordon Sumner is the real name of which musician and singer?
2. Who was President of Germany when Hitler came to power?
3. Who co-starred with Doris Day in a series of romantic comedies?
4. Which chemical element has the symbol Ag?
5. Which band had a 1983 hit with the song 'Gold'?
6. Where in Greece were the ancient Olympic Games held?
7. Who wrote the music for the film 'Chariots of Fire'?
8. What retail company was founded by Jeff Bezos in 1994?
9. Which cloud type takes its name from the Latin for heap?
10. Whose 'law states, 'If anything can go wrong, it will'?

Round 3

1. In Scottish and Irish surnames, what does Mac mean?
2. Which cartoon cat made its debut in 1919?
3. Which Australian brewer has varieties such as Pale Ale and Sparkling Ale?
4. Which city was captured by Saladin in 1187?
5. What was unique about Grover Cleveland's two terms as President of USA?
6. Which Asian city was founded by Sir Stamford Raffles in 1819?
7. Who created the Mr Men and Little Miss books?
8. How many US states begin with the letter O?
9. To which animal does the adjective caprine refer?
10. How many balls are used in eight ball pool?

Round 4

1. How many points is a touchdown worth in American football?
2. Captain Morgan and Lamb's are brands of which spirit?
3. Which country gained its independence from Ethiopia in 1993?
4. In which continent is the guava fruit indigenous?
5. In which country is Milford Sound?
6. Which team did literary character Roy of the Rovers play for?
7. In health, what does BMI stand for?
8. Who was Prime Minister of Australia when World War One broke out?
9. Who played Eliza Doolittle in the film version of My Fair Lady?
10. How many centimetres are there in a foot (nearest whole number)?

Round 5

1. Which small country is located between France and Spain?
2. What was the second film in The Matrix trilogy?
3. When sending an email, what does 'bcc' stand for?
4. Who directed The Shining?
5. What name is given the scale that grades wind speeds?
6. In which ocean would you find the Cape Verde Islands?
7. What is Spain's national sausage?
8. What is the capital of Barbados?
9. In which decade of the 19th century was the Crimean War fought?
10. What is the highest three digit prime number?

Quiz Forty Seven-Bonus Round Questions

1. Who led the Charge of the Light Brigade?
2. What was the band Queen's third album?
3. What is known as the 'Green Mountain State' in the US?

Answers Quiz Forty Seven

Round 1

1. Louis Armstrong
2. 540°
3. Lotus
4. Foo Fighters
5. Washington DC
6. Lesotho
7. Vincent
8. Attila the Hun
9. Lou Costello
10. Mahatma Ghandi

Round 2

1. Sting
2. Paul von Hindenburg
3. Rock Hudson
4. Silver
5. Spandau Ballet
6. Olympia
7. Vangelis
8. Amazon
9. Cumulus
10. Murphy's Law

Round 3

1. Son of
2. Felix
3. Coopers
4. Jerusalem
5. Not consecutive
6. Singapore
7. Roger Hargreaves
8. Three
9. Goat
10. 15 to be potted plus cue ball=16

Round 4

1. Six
2. Rum
3. Eritrea
4. South America
5. New Zealand
6. Melchester
7. Body Mass Index
8. Joseph Cook
9. Audrey Hepburn
10. 30

Round 5

1. Andorra
2. The Matrix Reloaded
3. Blind carbon copy
4. Stanley Kubrick
5. Beaufort Scale
6. Atlantic
7. Chorizo
8. Bridgetown
9. 1850s
10. 997

Quiz Forty Seven-Bonus Round Answers

1. Lord Cardigan
2. Sheer Heart Attack
3. Vermont

Quiz 48

Round 1

1. Who owned a pet snowy owl called Hedwig?
2. Cantaloupe and Honeydew are varieties of which fruit
3. Which zodiac sign is symbolised by a pair of scales?
4. Which historical character was played by Mel Gibson in 'Braveheart'?
5. Hibernia was the Roman name for which island?
6. What colour was the computer game character Pacman?
7. What flavour is Tia Maria liqueur?
8. How high in feet is the tennis net above the ground in the centre?
9. According to the proverb, what is the thief of time?
10. What takes about 8 minutes to travel from the Sun to Earth?

Round 2

1. Who did Mehmet Ali Agca attempt to assassinate in 1981?
2. Who won cricket's first World Cup in 1975?
3. In the Dr Doolittle stories, what sort of bird was Polynesia?
4. What divides the two main islands of New Zealand?
5. Who had a hit with 'Can the Can' in 1973?
6. Manuel II was the last king of which European country?
7. In which sport would you have left field and short stop?
8. What is the term for a kitchen on a ship or aircraft?
9. In Africa, what is a Harmattan?
10. Which letter is next: Z, X, C, V...?

Round 3

1. Richie Sambora is a guitarist in which band?
2. Who wrote the novel Myra Breckenridge?
3. What relation to King Arthur was Mordred?
4. In which Australian city is Taronga Park Zoo?
5. What four letter word can be found at the beginning of the name of over 30 Scottish whiskey distilleries?
6. What is the freezing point of water on the Fahrenheit scale?
7. Who wrote Wind in the Willows?
8. In rugby union, what position wears the number 9 shirt?
9. In which US state is the Kennedy Space Centre?
10. Who was the main foe of Robin Hood?

Round 4

1. Which of Henry VIII's wives was the last to die?
2. Who had a hit with the song 'I Feel Love'?
3. What is the surname of the family in the series 'Family Guy'?
4. What is arachnophobia?
5. What is the largest, in area, of Germany's states?
6. Which two animals appear on the coat of arms of Australia?
7. What is the anatomical name for the shoulder blade?
8. What substance is processed in a ginnery?
9. Which Dutch artist painted more than 90 self-portraits?
10. In which US city is Johns Hopkins University?

Round 5

1. How many US Vice Presidents have resigned from the post?
2. In Cluedo which is the only room to have a four letter name?
3. In which Asian country is Mandalay?
4. How many golfers play for each team in the Ryder Cup?
5. What were the first names of Mulder and Scully in 'The X-Files'?
6. 'Call me Ishmael' is the opening line in which well-known book?
7. What gas makes 21% of the Earth's atmosphere?
8. Linseed oil comes from which plant?
9. Which TV series was set at Wentworth Detention Centre?
10. Which pirate captained Queen Anne's Revenge?

Quiz Forty Eight-Bonus Round Questions

1. Which band had Demis Roussos on bass and vocals and Vangelis on keyboards?
2. Whose last words were, 'I am dying beyond my means'?
3. Which Egyptian God was killed by his bother Set?

Answers Quiz Forty Eight

Round 1

1. Harry Potter
2. Melon
3. Libra
4. William Wallace
5. Ireland
6. Yellow
7. Coffee
8. Three feet
9. Procrastination
10. Light

Round 2

1. Pope John Paul ll
2. West Indies
3. Parrot
4. Cook Strait
5. Suzi Quatro
6. Portugal
7. Baseball
8. Galley
9. A wind
10. B (bottom row on a Keyboard)

Round 3

1. Bon Jovi
2. Gore Vidal
3. Nephew
4. Sydney
5. Glen
6. 32°
7. Kenneth Grahame
8. Scrum half
9. Florida
10. Sheriff of Nottingham

Round 4

1. Anne of Cleves
2. Donna Summer
3. Griffin
4. A fear of spiders
5. Bavaria
6. Kangaroo & emu
7. Scapula
8. Cotton
9. Rembrandt
10. Baltimore

Round 5

1. Two
2. Hall
3. Burma (Myanmar)
4. 12
5. Fox and Dana
6. Moby Dick
7. Oxygen
8. Flax
9. Prisoner (Cell Block H)
10. Blackbeard (Edward Teach)

Quiz Forty Eight-Bonus Round Answers

1. Aphrodite's Child
2. Oscar Wilde
3. Osiris

Quiz 49

Round 1

1. The model Lesley Hornby became better known as whom?
2. What is the most populous city in Turkey?
3. Who wrote the book Dracula?
4. In what country is the budgerigar native?
5. What was the name of Sherlock Holmes' older brother?
6. Gaborone is the capital of which African country?
7. Who played the king in the 1956 film 'The King and I'?
8. Which band had a hit with Fanfare for the Common Man?
9. Which African country was formerly Called Upper Volta?
10. How many Formula One world titles did Michael Schumacher win?

Round 2

1. What is the longest athletics event, in distance, at the Olympics and world Championships?
2. What was the sequel to the film, Honey I Shrunk the Kids?
3. Who wrote the song I'm A Believer?
4. What was first played at Kennington Oval on 16th March 1872?
5. Who was Sebastian Vettel's team-mate at Red Bull in Formula One from 2009 to 2013?
6. In Indian cooking, what is ghee?
7. In the TV series Dallas, who was JR Ewing's wife?
8. What was the real first name of King George VI?
9. Who created Winnie the Pooh?
10. In which American state is Jim Beam distilled?

Round 3

1. Grevy's is the largest species of which equine mammal?
2. Who was Propaganda Minister in Nazi Germany?
3. Bratislava is the capital of which country?
4. What are the favourite flowers of Dame Edna Everage?
5. Who had a hit in 1977 with the song 'Pearl's a Singer'?
6. Which prehistoric monster first menaced Tokyo in a 1954 film?
7. What was John Lennon's original middle name?
8. What nationality was Adolphe Sax, the inventor of the saxophone?
9. In which country was revolutionary Che Guevara killed?
10. What is the capital of Tasmania?

Round 4

1. Which musical play and film is based around the songs of ABBA?
2. What is a male goose called?
3. From which Italian region do Chianti wines come from?
4. Which Polish composer wrote 51 mazurkas?
5. Who was the girlfriend of Superman?
6. What flavour is the German drink kirsch?
7. The Gulf of Aqaba is an inlet to which sea?
8. In what year were the Dead Sea Scrolls found?
9. Which sport do the Illawarra Hawks play?
10. Which Ancient Greek scientist famously said 'Eureka' while in the bath?

Round 5

1. Who is the next door neighbour of the Simpsons?
2. Which species of dung beetle was sacred to Ancient Egyptians?
3. An excess of which acid in the blood causes gout?
4. What are stuffed in Greek cuisine to make dolmades?
5. In the Odyssey, who was the wife of Odysseus?
6. Which actor's first film was Citizen Kane?
7. Who sang the song 'Fields of Gold'?
8. What does it mean if you are faced with Hobson's choice?
9. What is the capital of Croatia?
10. Which character did Eddie Murphy voice in the Shrek movies?

Quiz Forty Nine-Bonus Round Questions

1. Which crime writer also used the name Barbara Vine for her works?
2. Which actor appears on the Queen single 'Flash' going 'Gordon's Alive'?
3. Which hereditary honour was instituted by James I in 1611?

Answers Quiz Forty Nine

Round 1

1. Twiggy
2. Istanbul
3. Bram Stoker
4. Australia
5. Mycroft
6. Botswana
7. Yul Brynner
8. Emerson, Lake & Palmer
9. Burkina Faso
10. Seven

Round 2

1. 50km walk
2. Honey I Blew Up the Kid
3. Neil Diamond
4. FA Cup final
5. Mark Webber
6. Clarified butter
7. Sue Ellen
8. Albert
9. AA Milne
10. Kentucky

Round 3

1. Zebra
2. Joseph Goebbels
3. Slovakia
4. Gladioli
5. Elkie Brooks
6. Godzilla
7. Winston
8. Belgian
9. Bolivia
10. Hobart

Round 4

1. Mamma Mia
2. Gander
3. Tuscany
4. Chopin
5. Lois Lane
6. Cherry
7. Red Sea
8. 1947
9. Basketball
10. Archimedes

Round 5

1. Ned Flanders
2. Scarab
3. Uric acid
4. Vine leaves
5. Penelope
6. Orson Welles
7. Sting
8. You don't have a choice
9. Zagreb
10. Donkey

Quiz Forty Nine-Bonus Round Answers

1. Ruth Rendell
2. Brian Blessed
3. Baronet

Quiz 50

Round 1

1. What, in the Bible was built from gopherwood?
2. Which insect has the scientific name Musca Domestica?
3. What word is formed by the Roman numeral for 1009?
4. In animation, who was chased by Tweety Pie?
5. Which Scottish liqueur was said to be the favourite of Bonnie Prince Charlie?
6. Sookie Stackhouse is a leading character in which TV series?
7. What instrument did musician Nat 'King' Cole play?
8. Which company made the Brownie camera?
9. Which song by George Ezra is also the capital of Hungary?
10. Near which Australian state is the Great Barrier Reef?

Round 2

1. Which musician was backed by the MGs?
2. Which organ of the body is affected by Bright's disease?
3. A roaring lion is the trademark for which film company?
4. What colour is the rock azurite?
5. Nick Leeson was responsible for the collapse of which bank?
6. In which city does the International Court of Justice sit?
7. Who famously rode from Boston to Lexington in 1775?
8. What name is given to angle between 180 and 360 degrees?
9. From which French wine region does claret come from?
10. Nobody Does it Better was the theme song for which James Bond film?

Round 3

1. Which former Neighbours star had a hit with 'Torn'?
2. In which American state is Nantucket?
3. Which sport takes place at a Basho?
4. Who established the Legion of Honour in France in 1802?
5. In which year was the Wall Street crash?
6. Which outlaw was killed by Pat Garrett?
7. Which singer had a backing band called the Crickets?
8. What is the English name for zucchini?
9. 50° Fahrenheit is how many degrees in Celsius?
10. Who did the CIA try to assassinate with an exploding cigar?

Round 4

1. Ace of Base and Roxette are bands from which country?
2. Who is the creator of the Horrible Histories books?
3. Who wrote Lady Chatterley's Lover?
4. Where was the setting for Fawlty Towers?
5. Blood and Fire is the motto for which organisation?
6. What Nestle product does George Clooney advertise?
7. Scott Joplin was a composer of what form of music?
8. What ritual dance is performed by the All Blacks prior to a rugby match?
9. Where in New York State is the United States Military Academy based?
10. Which is the heaviest of the three swords used in fencing?

Round 5

1. Galena is the most common ore for which metal?
2. Which two numbers are on either side of the 20 on a dart board?
3. In Morse code which letter is represented by two dots?
4. Which tennis player was nicknamed 'The Iceberg'?
5. What was the name of the third Mad Max film?
6. Which TV cat caused trouble for Officer Dibble?
7. Night blindness is caused by a deficiency of which vitamin?
8. How many nanometres in a metre?
9. Who was the first Emperor of China from the Yuan Dynasty in 1279?
10. Where did Jean Shrimpton famously wear a mini skirt in 1965?

Quiz Fifty-Bonus Round Questions

1. How many cervical vertebrae does a human have?
2. Who is the father of Viscount Severn?
3. In what year was the Encyclopaedia Britannica first published?

Answers Quiz Fifty

Round 1

1. Noah's Ark
2. House fly
3. MIX
4. Sylvester
5. Drambuie
6. True Blood
7. Piano
8. Kodak
9. Budapest
10. Queensland

Round 2

1. Booker T
2. Kidney
3. MGM
4. Blue
5. Baring's Bank
6. The Hague
7. Paul Revere
8. Reflex
9. Bordeaux
10. The Spy Who Loved Me

Round 3

1. Natalie Imbruglia
2. Massachusetts
3. Sumo wrestling
4. Napoleon Bonaparte
5. 1929
6. Billy the Kid
7. Buddy Holly
8. Courgette
9. 10 degrees
10. Fidel Castro

Round 4

1. Sweden
2. Terry Deary
3. DH Lawrence
4. Torquay
5. Salvation Army
6. Nespresso
7. Ragtime
8. Haka
9. West Point
10. Epee

Round 5

1. Lead
2. 5 and 1
3. I
4. Bjorn Borg
5. Mad Max Beyond Thunderdome
6. Top Cat
7. Vitamin A
8. One billion
9. Kublai Khan
10. Melbourne Cup

Quiz Fifty-Bonus Round Answers

1. Seven
2. Prince Edward
3. 1768

True Or False

The first test cricket match was played in England **F** Australia

North Macedonia is in Europe **T**

The oldest toilet seat was found in Syria   **F** Egypt

The women's World Cup of cricket has not been held in New Zealand   **F**

Uma Thurman has been married twice   **T**

Maureen Connolly was a famous tennis player   **T**

The Nile is the world's longest river **T**

The Adelaide Crows began in the AFL in 1992   **F** 1991

Rowan Atkinson starred in 4 series of Blackadder **T**

Fitzroy won 6 premierships in the VFL   **F** 8

The Sound of Music was set in Germany   **F** Austria

Greg Chappell has scored the most runs for Australia in test cricket   **F** Allan Border

The 1896 Athens Olympic Games were opened by Baron Pierre de Coubertin   **F** King George I of Greece

The next star sign after Capricorn is Aquarius   **F**   Sagittarius

The comic The Phantom was written by Lee Falk **T**

The Battle of the Somme in WWI was in 1916   **T**

The President of South Africa is Nelson Mandela **F**

The song Sheena Is a Punk Rocker was by the Ramones **T**

The youngest of the Three Stooges was Curly   **T**

The world's heaviest twins were 11.9 kg when they were born **F**   12.6 kg

Thomas Wedders had a nose that measured 19 cm long **T**

The longest stay on Mt Everest was 21 hours   **T**

The world's longest kiss lasted 26 hours   **F** 30 hrs 45 mins

The fastest haircut took 1 min 13 sec   **T**

The most people that have danced to YMCA is 5638 people   **F** 6907

Apart from the sun, the nearest star to Earth is 4.74 light years away   **F** 4.23 light years

The largest moon in the solar system is Europa   **F**   Ganymede

The world's largest volcano is in Asia **F**   South America

The warmest year on record was in 1998   **T**

The most powerful Earthquake measured 9.4 on the Richter Scale   **T**

The largest land mammal is the male Indian elephant   **F** African elephant

There are around 1560 species of flea   **F** 1830

The oldest cat lived to 34 years of age **T**

Mexico City is the world's most polluted city   F   Linchen China
Argentina eats the most beef in the world   T
The world's oldest prisoner was 98 when he died in 1989 F   108
China has the largest army in the world   T
The worlds worst train disaster was in 1981   T
Ghandi is the most expensive film ever made   F   Titanic
Actress Katherine Hepburn gave an Oscar speech for 5 minutes 30 seconds   F   Greer Garson
The West Wing won 9 Emmy Awards in 1999   T
The Beatles first song was recorded in 1963   F   1962
The largest telescope weighs 3218 kg   F   2998 kg
There are 270 stations on the London Underground   T
The busiest airport in the world is Hartsfield Airport in Georgia USA   T
Radio City Music Hall in New York has 5910 seats T
The Washington Redskins scored 71 points in a game of gridiron   F
73 points
Michael Jordan has scored the most points in the NBA   F   Kareem Abdul Jabbar
Elvis Presley had 18 No. 1 hits T
The album Rumours by Fleetwood Mac was released in 1977 T
Author Agatha Christie has sold 2 billion copies of her books   T
The Statue of Liberty stands 87.89 m   F   92.99m
The most expensive animation film is The Lion King   F Tangled
The largest jigsaw puzzle has 20000 pieces F   40000 pieces
The largest lottery prize in Australia was $158 million   F $110 million
The largest hotel is in New York   F   Las Vegas
The HMS Victory took 5 years to build   F   6 years
Baseballer Nolan Ryan struck out 5714 batters in his career   T
Manchester United are the most valuable soccer team in the world   T
The smallest returning boomerang measures 48 mm long   T
The Battle of the Somme lasted 142 days   T
The most successful Australian film is Mad Max   F   Crocodile Dundee
The solar car Solar Star recorded a highest speed of 125 kmh   F   135kmh
The tallest chimney measures 420 m tall   T
The largest shopping centre is in Los Angeles   F   Edmonton Canada

The United States has won the most Davis Cups in tennis   **T**

The longest tennis match lasted 5 hrs 31 min   **T**

The most gold medals won by one country at on Olympic Games is 83   **T**

Cy Young was a famous ice hockey player   **F**   Baseball

Roy Berger did 2674 push ups in one hour   **F**   3416

The longest solar eclipse lasted 6 min 54 sec   **F**   7 min 8 sec

A rainbow once lasted for 6 hours in England   **T**

The tallest cactus is in Arizona   **F**   Mexico

The Great White Shark weighs up to 770 kg   **T**

The longest time spent in solitary confinement in a prison is 12 years **T**

Tommy Johns was arrested 2000 times   **F**   Nearly 3000 times

The biggest grossing western film is Dances With Wolves   **T**

Hey Jude by The Beatles was No. 1 on the Australian charts for 12 weeks
        F   15 weeks

The Lion King is the highest grossing animated film   **F**   Frozen 2

The largest airships were 245 m long   **T**

United Airlines is the busiest airline in the world   **F**   American
Airlines

The CN Tower in Toronto is 553 m tall   **T**

The Chicago Bulls won 72 games in one season   **T**

Roy Sullivan survived 7 lightning strikes on him   **T**

The youngest Oscar winner was 13 years old   **F**   10 yrs old

The oldest winner of an Oscar was 80 yrs old   **T**

The most successful country singer is Garth Brooks   **T**

Bill Clinton appeared on the front cover of Time Magazine 55 times   **F**
        Richard Nixon

The Pope was elected to the position in 1981   **F**   1978

The most expensive private jet is $500 million   **T**

A blue whale can weigh up to 130 tonnes   **T**

In 1981 over 400 people were killed by piranhas   **F**   over 300

A goldfish has lived to 43 years T

A South African sharp nosed frog jumped 10.3 m in 3 jumps   **T**

The longest scarf knitted was 174 m long   **T**

The largest collection of wine labels is 12453   **F**   Over 15400

There are over 125 million items in the US Library of Congress   **T**

The longest running TV show is Coronation St   **F**   Meet The Press

Savage Garden's first album sold 11 million copies **T**

The pianist Liberace earned $125000 for a single night's performance   **F**
        $138000

Zorro has been portrayed in 69 films   **T**

The fastest speed of a kite was 193 kmh   **T**

Magic Kingdom in Disneyworld Florida is the most visited theme park in the world   **T**

The most number of people in space at the same time is 16   **F**   13

The USA has the most nuclear submarines in its fleet   **T**

The most expensive motorcycle is priced at $7 900 000   **F** $11 million

Pete Rose has played the most games of baseball in the Major League   **T**

The Dallas Cowboys have won the most Super Bowl titles   **F**   New England/Pittsburgh

The Stanley Cup is awarded in golf   **F**   Ice hockey

Ben Hogan was a famous basketball player   **F**   Golf player

Austria has won the most medals at the Winter Olympics   **F**   Norway

The lowest score in a test cricket match is 26   **T**   New Zealand

Port Adelaide has won 36 Premierships in the SANFL   **T**

The most valuable deck of cards is worth $125000   **F** $143352

Seven actors have won the Best Director Award at the Academy Awards   **F**   5

Tie Breaker Questions

The Spanish Eurovision entry in 1986 entitled La, La, La contained how many la`s? **138**

How many years in prison did the 12 members of the Great Train Robbery gang get between them in 1964? **307**

In what year was the Cutty Sark built? **1869**

In what year was the film Chitty Chitty Bang Bang released? **1968**

In what year did Madame Tussaud`s first open? **1928**

To the nearest whole number, what percentage of the Earth's atmosphere is nitrogen? **78%**

In what year was the country of Siam renamed Thailand? **1939**

In what year did Rio de Janeiro cease to be the capital of Brazil? **1960**

In what year was DNA discovered? **1953**

In what year was the hot air balloon invented? **1783**

In what year did Laszlo Biro invent the ballpoint pen? **1946**

How many times did Nigel Mansell win the British Grand Prix? **4**

How many muscles does a cat have in each ear? **32**

On what date was Mickey Mouse born? **November 18 1928**

How many times are the words `Love Shack` mentioned in the B-52s hit of the same name? **40**

In what year was `Pong`, the first ever video game released? **1972**

How many days is the average gestation period of a mouse? **21**

In what year did the first execution by lethal injection take place in America? **1982**

As at January 1st, 2019, how many Popes have been assassinated? **26**

When was the Barbie doll first sold with bendable legs? **1965**

In inches what is the diameter of a standard dartboard? **18 inches**

By how many days did Amundsen beat Scott to become the first person to reach the South Pole? **35**

In what year was barbed wire invented? **1874**

In which decade did the two-man bobsled team begin competing at the world level? **1930s**

How many feature films did Alfred Hitchcock direct which had only one word in the title? **15**

How many tiles are used in the game Mah-jong? **144**

In what year did George de Mestral invent Velcro? **1955**

When was the game of Monopoly invented? **1932**

How many books are in the Bible? **66**

To what speed does the car in `Back To The Future` have to reach to travel in time? **88 miles per hour**

In which century did Good King Wenceslas live? **10th**

When was the first Tour De France bike race contested? **1903**

Fairview is the most common name for a city in America. How many cities are named this? **66**

In which year was the Irish political party, Sinn Fein formed? **1905**

In what year were the Grammy Awards first awarded? **1959**

How many Oscars did the film `West Side Story` win? **10**

How many fences are jumped in the Grand National? **30**

How many feet wide is a basketball court? **50**

In what year was the safety pin invented? **1849**

How many centimetres long is a cricket bail? **11**

How many storeys high is Sears Tower in America? **110**

How many islands are in Fiji? **332**

In the film starring Tom Hanks, what is Forrest Gump`s I.Q.? **75**

How tall is the Eiffel Tower in metres? **322m**

How many different roles does Alec Guinness play in `Kind Hearts And Coronets`? **8**

In which year was the comic strip character of Popeye created? **1929**

How many years elapsed between the Wright brothers` first flight and Neil Armstrong`s walk on the Moon? **66**

In the year 1900, what was the average age at death of people in America? **47**

In what year was Morse code devised? **1832**

In what year was the first Cannes Film Festival held? **1946**

How many stories make up the `Canterbury Tales`? **24**

In which year did London`s first airport open? **1919**

How many white five pointed stars are there on the Brazilian flag? **27**

How many pods are on the Millennium Eye in London? **32**

In what year was Coca Cola first sold in bottles? **1894**

How many countries border Germany? **9**

In which year was the first London marathon run? **1981**

How many league goals did Ally McCoist score for Rangers between the years 1985 and 1998? **355**

How many steps are there in the Eiffel Tower? **1,792**

For how many million years did the Jurassic period last? **180 million**

How many UK number one singles has Cliff Richard had? **13**

In which year did the first Alcoholics Anonymous first meeting take place? **1935**

In which year did Coca Cola introduce Cherry Coke? **1985**

What was the common age of Jimi Hendrix, Janis Joplin and Jim Morrison when they died? **27**

In which year was Burger King founded? **1954**

How many vowels are there in the Greek alphabet? **7**

What score is needed in an IQ test to be in the top 1% of the population? **155**

In what year did the first cricket Test match take place between Australia and England? **1877**

For how many years did Louis XIV of France reign? **72**

How old was Tatum O`Neal when she received the Best Supporting Actress Oscar for the film `Paper Moon`? **10**

In which year was a test cricket match tied for the first time? **1960**

In what year did the first bikini go on show at a Paris fashion show? **1946**

How old was Queen Victoria when she ascended the throne in 1837? **18**

In which year was the film studio Paramount opened? **1912**

How many films did Elvis Presley star in? **33**

In what year was the first FA Cup final held at Wembley? **1923**

How many countries took place in the 1996 Olympic Games? **197**

In which year were bar codes first introduced into shops in America? **1974**

How many events were contested in the first ever Olympic Games? **43**

At what age did Marilyn Monroe die? **36**

In which decade was insulin first used to treat Diabetes? **1920s**

How many islands make up the Maldives? **1196**

In kilometres, how long is the Suez Canal? **161.9 km**

When was Lewis Carroll`s book `Alice`s Adventures in Wonderland` written? **1865**

What is the Fahrenheit equivalent of 20 degrees centigrade? **68**

How old was Tiger Woods when he won the US Masters in 1997? **21**

In what year was the first Miss World contest held? **1951**

How old was Buddy Holly when he died in a plane crash in 1959? **22**

What number on the Beaufort scale represents a storm? **10**

In what year did the first recorded railroad accident occur? **1832**

How many spots in total does a full standard set of dominos have? **168**

In what year was the world`s first daily newspaper published? **1702**

How many characters are there in the Russian alphabet? **33**

In millimetres, what is the width of an A10 sheet of paper? **26**

How many episodes of Friends were there? **236**

How many studio albums did John Denver record? **30**

How many nations fought in World War One? **32**

How many nations fought in the Korean War? **25**

How many episodes were there of the TV series Hogan's Heroes? **168**

How many studio albums were recorded by the Beach Boys? **29**

Quiz Night

Team Name: _____

Round: _____

Q	Answer
1	
2	
3	
4	
5	
6	
7	
8	
9	
10	

Bonus Questions	
1.	
2.	
3.	

Quiz Night

Team Name: _____

Round: _____

Q	Answer
1	
2	
3	
4	
5	
6	
7	
8	
9	
10	

Lightning Source UK Ltd.
Milton Keynes UK
UKHW050626210922
409198UK00004B/479